SPECTRUM

Reading

Grade 2

Spectrum
An imprint of Carson-Dellosa Publishing LLC
P.O. Box 35665
Greensboro, NC 27425 USA

Printed in the USA • All rights reserved.   ISBN 978-0-7696-3862-1

04-087117811

Index of Skills

Reading Grade 2

Numerals indicate the exercise pages on which these skills appear.

Vocabulary Skills

Abbreviations 81

Antonyms 11, 51, 65, 89, 117, 125, 149

Base Words and Endings 7, 23, 43, 67, 93, 127, 147

Blends 17, 23, 41, 87, 109, 139

Classification 13, 27, 61, 85, 111, 141

Compound Words 19, 31, 41, 69, 99, 137

Consonant Digraphs 45, 61, 91, 119, 145

Contractions 15, 43, 67, 95, 127, 151

Decode Multisyllable Words 59, 103, 133

Final Consonants 9, 29, 65, 93, 123, 151

Initial Consonants 13, 31, 79, 107, 139

Irregular Spellings 63

Long Vowels 25, 49, 83, 115, 143

Meaning From Context 3, 5, 15, 21, 27, 37, 39, 47, 53, 63, 79, 89, 97, 115, 125, 129, 131, 145, 147

Multiple Meanings 25, 39, 47, 57, 73, 91, 135

Possessives 35, 83, 107, 131

Prefixes and Suffixes 45, 73, 99, 103, 121

R-Controlled Vowels 53, 77, 121, 143

Rhyming Words 29, 37, 55, 87, 105, 135

Short Vowels 21, 57, 69, 75, 101, 129

Singular and Plural 5, 33, 49, 63, 81, 109, 123, 149

Syllables 55, 85, 117, 145

Synonyms 33, 51, 71, 95, 119, 147

Variant Sounds 71, 133

Vowel Digraphs and Diphthongs 35, 59, 77, 97, 113, 141

Reading Skills

Ask Clarifying Questions 29, 87, 117

Cause and Effect 13, 43, 59, 65, 69, 113, 119, 129, 141

Character Analysis 9, 41, 67, 107, 115, 137

Comparison and Contrast 31, 61, 77, 103

Context Clues 19, 57 61, 73, 91, 109, 127, 137, 143

Drawing Conclusions 3, 9, 45, 47, 57, 63, 79, 99, 101, 121, 123, 133, 143, 147

Facts and Details 3, 15, 21, 25, 27, 35, 45, 49, 69, 77, 89, 95, 101, 113, 123, 125, 141, 135, 145

Give Purpose for Reading all activity pages

Identify Purpose of Text (inform, entertain) 5, 17, 31, 89, 97, 131

Identify Supporting Information 7, 41, 59, 67, 73, 95, 121, 143, 151

Main Idea 5, 13, 23, 29, 33, 39, 47, 69, 77, 83, 91, 97, 101, 109, 123, 125, 139, 145, 147

Picture Clues 15, 25, 55, 63, 93, 119, 137, 151

Predicting Outcomes 23, 27, 55, 67, 85, 115, 129, 135

Reality and Fantasy 53, 65, 93, 99, 141

Recognize Story's Problem 105, 135

Sequence 11, 49, 53, 71, 75, 81, 105, 111, 131, 145

Understand and Identify Simple Literature Terms 97, 135

Understand That Word Choice Can Shape Ideas, Feelings, and Actions 83, 117, 129

Use Prior Knowledge 5, 17, 31, 89, 97, 131

Word Referents 23, 57, 79, 133

Study Skills

Alphabetical Order 19, 37, 75, 101, 107, 147

Following Directions all activity pages

Interpret Information—diagrams, graphs, charts 71, 85, 111, 113, 125

Use Titles, TOC, Headings to Locate Information 17, 33, 61, 63, 103, 139, 151

Table of Contents

Dad's First Day

Read to see why Dad is upset.

1   I think Dad is nervous. At breakfast, he almost poured milk into his orange juice instead of into his cereal bowl! Mom doesn't seem worried. She knows why Dad is a little upset. Today is his first day at a new job.

2   My dad builds bridges. Some of them look heavy and strong. Others look light, as if they are just hanging in the air. Dad says the light bridges are just as strong as the heavy ones.

3   Dad is an excellent bridge builder, even at home. Once, we almost filled my whole room with bridges. We used boxes, blocks, pots, pans, and even the dog's dish. It was great.

4   I know Dad has tons of great bridge ideas, so he shouldn't be nervous. I guess he just wants to practice making one more bridge before he goes to work.

Vocabulary Skills

Write the words from the story that have these meanings.

1. jumpy

_____
(Par. 1)

2. very, very good

_____
(Par. 3)

3. to repeat an action

_____
(Par. 4)

Reading Skills

1. What kinds of bridges does Dad build?

_____

_____

2. Why is Dad nervous?

_____

_____

3. How does the boy know that Dad is nervous?

_____

_____

4. What kind of bridge did the boy and Dad make at home?

_____

_____

Bridges

What kinds of bridges are there?

1   Have you ever stepped on a stone to get across a puddle or stream? If you have, you were using a bridge.

2   Bridges are different sizes and shapes. Some bridges have straight "legs," or supports, called *beams*. Other bridges have curved supports, called *arches*. Still others actually hang from strong steel ropes, or cables, that are strung above the surface of the bridge. The cables are then attached to the land on either end of the bridge.

3   Most bridges go over water, but some bridges were made to carry water. About 2,000 years ago, the Romans built this kind of bridge. One such bridge, in France, had three levels. Water flowed in the top level, and people and carts traveled on the two lower levels.

Vocabulary Skills

Add **s** to a word to show more than one.

1. one bridge

two _____

2. one beam

two _____

3. one cable

many _____

4. one year

eight _____

Circle the best word for each sentence. Then, write it in the blank.

5. A bridge's supports might be called its _____.

arms   legs   eyes

6. A bridge with curves underneath has _____.

arches   cables   beams

Reading Skills

1. This passage is mostly about

_____ old bridges.

_____ kinds of bridges.

_____ making bridges.

2. The author wrote this selection to

_____ make you laugh.

_____ help you learn.

3. Think about what you already know about bridges. What are bridges for?

_____

_____

4. This passage tells about another use for bridges. What is it?

_____

_____

Bridges to Remember

Read to find out what is special about these bridges.

1 Some people do not like to drive across bridges. They look straight ahead and try to hold their breath until they get to the other side. Good luck if those people are driving in Louisiana. There is a 24-mile-long bridge there! It takes about half an hour to get across.

2 If you like to look way, way down when you cross a bridge, you should go to Colorado. A bridge there stands more than a thousand feet above a river. A 75-story building could fit under that bridge!

3 If you do not like to look down, get in the middle lane of a bridge in Australia. It has eight lanes for cars, two train tracks, a bike path, and a sidewalk.

4 Finally, if you like crowds and bridges, go to India. A bridge there carries 100,000 cars and trucks every day, plus thousands of walkers.

Vocabulary Skills

The words *walked, walks,* and *walking* all have the same base word, *walk*. Write the base word for each set of words below.

1. looks, looked, looking

   _____

2. crossing, crossed, crosses

   _____

3. driven, drives, driving

   _____

4. carries, carried, carrying

   _____

Reading Skills

1. How does the text help you understand how long a 24-mile-long bridge is?

   _____

   _____

2. How does the text help you understand how high the bridge in Colorado is?

   _____

   _____

3. If you do not like to look over the side of a bridge, why would the bridge in Australia be a good one to cross?

   _____

   _____

4. Why is the bridge in India a bridge to remember?

   _____

   _____

   _____

Moving-Out Day

Read to see how Emily feels about moving.

1   *There goes another box,* thought Emily. *All my stuff is in boxes. It's all getting squashed together.*

2   Mom stood on the front steps. "Oh, be careful with that one!" she cried. The movers nodded as they went past. *All my stuff is in boxes,* thought Mom. *It might all get broken.*

3   Dad came out of the garage. "Wow, this is a heavy one! It might break everything else." Mom and Emily frowned.

4   An hour later, the boxes were still going past. One box had holes in it. Emily had made the holes so her stuffed animals could get some air.

5   Finally, they all watched the movers close up the truck. *Ka-thunk* went the big doors. Dad gave Emily a little hug. "One empty house and one full truck. That's a good day's work."

Vocabulary Skills

The missing word in each sentence ends with an **s**. Write the correct word in the blank.

1. The movers carried many heavy brown _____.

2. Emily made _____ in one box.

3. Emily thought her stuffed _____ might need air.

Reading Skills

1. What do Mom and Emily worry about?

_____

_____

2. Circle the word that best tells how Emily feels about her stuffed animals.

hopeless   caring   harsh

3. What word best tells how Mom feels? Circle it.

relaxed   worried   careless

4. How do you think Dad feels about moving day?

_____

_____

5. What clues in the story help you know how Dad feels?

_____

_____

Moving-In Day

What does Emily think of her new home?

1   "Emily, would you go turn on the lights, please?" asked Mom. "The movers will need to see when they bring our stuff in."

2   "Sure, Mom." Emily was happy to check out the new house. She turned on twelve lights, then went back to Mom.

3   "Why don't you help me unpack this box?" asked Mom.

4   "Sure, Mom," said Emily.

5   Mom and Emily lifted out shapes wrapped in newspaper. One was the cookie jar. Another was a mug. Then, Mom unwrapped a roll of paper.

6   "Oh, look, Emily! It's the picture you drew last summer!" Emily saw the picture she had made of her family. They were all smiling. The picture made Emily smile, even here in the new house.

7   Mom smiled, too. "Let's put it on the refrigerator," they said together. And they did.

Vocabulary Skills

The meanings of *new* and *old* are opposite. Make a line from each word in the first list to a word in the second list with the opposite meaning.

1. unhappy   frown

2. on   summer

3. winter   glad

4. smile   off

Reading Skills

1. Why was Emily happy to go turn on the lights?

_____

_____

2. How did the picture make Emily feel?

_____

_____

3. How did Emily feel about her new house?

_____

_____

4. Write 1, 2, and 3 by these sentences to show what happened first, next, and last.

_____ Emily turned on the lights.

_____ Mom and Emily put a picture on the refrigerator.

_____ Mom and Emily unpacked a box.

Boxes, Books, and More

How do Emily's feelings about the new house change?

1   Emily pushed a box across the floor. Her room was so empty! She didn't like it. Her old room had been pink. This one was just plain white.

2   Emily's mom poked her head in. "Do you need any help?"

3   "No, I'm okay, Mom. I'm going to unpack my books first."

4   "That sounds good," said Mom. "I'll just make up your bed. Okay?"

5   "Thanks, Mom." Emily put the biggest books on the bottom shelf. She put the medium books on the middle shelf. She put the smallest books on the top shelf. It took a long time because she stopped to read some of them along the way.

6   Emily stepped back. All of her books were in place. Her quilt was on her bed. Everything looked just right.

NAME _____

Vocabulary Skills

Circle the three words in each line that belong together.

1. green   book   white   blue

2. skip   walk   run   shoe

3. tree   bed   pillow   lamp

4. big   top   small   medium

Circle the best word for each sentence. Then, write it in the blank.

5. Emily's new room is
   _____.

   pink   park   plain

6. Emily put her _____ on a shelf.

   bed   books   boxes

7. Emily's mom put a
   _____ on the bed.

   quick   quilt   quiet

Reading Skills

1. This story is mostly about

   _____ Emily's new room.

   _____ how busy Mom is.

   _____ Emily's toys.

2. At the beginning of the story, what does Emily think about her new room?

   _____

   _____

3. What does Emily think of her room at the end of the story?

   _____

   _____

4. What happened to change Emily's feelings?

   _____

   _____

   _____

No Boxes Today

Read to see what Emily learns about her new home.

1 "Who is tired of unpacking boxes?" asked Dad at breakfast. Mom and Emily laughed and raised their hands high.

2 "Why don't we go on a little tour? We won't even think about boxes today," said Dad.

3 "What will we tour, Dad?" asked Emily.

4 "We'll tour our new city. San Antonio is an exciting place."

5 "Are there old houses?" asked Emily. She liked old houses.

6 "Yes, there are, but I thought we might start at the Children's Museum."

7 Emily grinned. "There is a museum just for me? Wow!"

8 "And after that," said Dad, "we can ride in a river taxi."

9 "Okay, let's go!" said Emily, jumping up from the table.

10 Mom and Dad laughed. "Maybe you should get dressed first, Emily."

Vocabulary Skills

Sometimes a shorter word is used to stand for two other words. Write the shorter word from the box that stands for the underlined words in each sentence.

don't	let's
won't	we'll

1. <u>Let us</u> get ready to go.

   _____

2. We <u>will not</u> unpack today.

   _____

3. I think <u>we will</u> have a good time.

   _____

4. We <u>do not</u> want to miss the taxi.

   _____

Write the story words that have these meanings.

5. worn out

   _____
   (Par. 1)

6. town

   _____
   (Par. 4)

7. to begin

   _____
   (Par. 6)

8. a flowing body of water

   _____
   (Par. 8)

Reading Skills

Look at each picture and circle the sentence that goes with it.

1. Emily is eating breakfast.

   Emily is making her bed.

2. Dad is carrying a box.

   Dad is unpacking a box.

3. What meal is the family eating?

   _____

4. Why can't the family leave right away?

   _____

The Texas Story

What do you know about Texas? Read to see what else you can learn.

How Big Is Texas?

1 Texas is the second-largest state in the United States. Only Alaska is larger. Texas is also second when it comes to the number of people living in the state. Only California has more people than Texas.

How Old Is Texas?

2 On December 29, 1845, Texas became a state. It was the twenty-eighth state. In 2005, Texas was 160 years old.

What Comes From Texas?

3 The huge state of Texas gives us many things to eat and use. Many farmers raise cattle for beef and milk. Other farmers grow grapefruit, which is Texas's state fruit.

4 There is much oil in Texas. Once oil is drilled out of the ground, it is used to make many things, including gas for our cars and plastic.

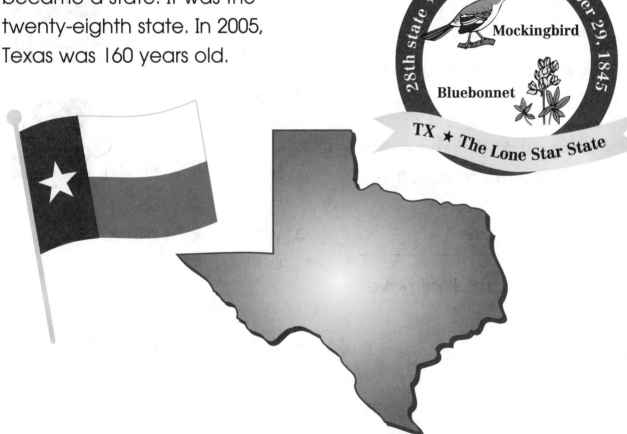

28th state ★ Statehood: December 29, 1845
Mockingbird
Bluebonnet
TX ★ The Lone Star State

Vocabulary Skills

Circle the best word for each sentence. Then, write it in the blank.

1. Texas is a large

   _____.

   start   salt   state

2. Grapefruit is a large yellow

   _____.

   frame   fruit   flow

3. Have you seen a grapefruit

   _____?

   grab   growing   green

4. Oil is _____ from the ground.

   drilled   drink   droop

Reading Skills

1. What did you know about Texas?

   _____

   _____

2. List two new things you learned about Texas.

   _____

   _____

3. What question would you like to ask about Texas?

   _____

   _____

4. Why do you think the author wrote this article about Texas?

   _____ to help me learn something

   _____ to make me laugh

Study Skills

A **heading** is a short title that gives a clue about something that comes next.

1. Under what heading might you find the size of Texas?

   _____

2. Under what heading might you find the age of Texas?

   _____

San Antonio Today

Do you think you would like to visit San Antonio?

¹ In San Antonio today, a visitor can learn many things about Texas's past. Many old buildings still stand. At the same time, it is a modern city. People visit San Antonio to eat, shop, go to concerts, and see the sights. The city's River Walk is a common place to go. The San Antonio River flows right through downtown. Along the river are many shops and hotels. Beautiful plants grow along the River Walk, too. Many bridges and stairways help people get from one place to another.

² If you don't feel like walking, you might choose to ride a streetcar. You can see all of downtown and the River Walk from your seat. Or, if you like the water, you can take a river taxi. River taxis travel all along the 21 blocks of the River Walk.

Vocabulary Skills

Read each sentence and circle the word that is made of two shorter words. Write the two words on the lines.

1. To go up, use a stairway.

_____ _____

2. It's fun to ride a streetcar.

_____ _____

3. The river runs through downtown.

_____ _____

Reading Skills

Write each word in the correct blank.

city	concert
hotels	ride

1. If you like music, go to a _____.

2. San Antonio is a large, modern _____.

3. If you are tired, _____ in a river taxi.

4. People sleep in _____ along the River Walk.

Study Skills

Write each set of words in A-B-C order.

1. many   visit   stand

_____
_____
_____

2. place   grow   flows

_____
_____
_____

3. like   taxi   from

_____
_____
_____

Paul Bunyan: A New Story

Read this tall tale to find out how Paul Bunyan solves a problem.

1   After the great race, everyone in Minnesota was wondering what to do about all the holes that Paul and Babe's feet had made. In fact, they were sort of angry about all those holes. They said they couldn't plow their fields or walk through the woods any more. Every time they tried, they fell into one of those holes. Paul felt terrible, but Babe felt so badly that he ran away. The next day, Paul climbed the Black Hills to see if he could see Babe. Then, he looked under the Mississippi River, but Babe wasn't there.

2   At the end of the day, Paul just sat down and cried. He cried so hard that all of those holes filled up with water. The people in Minnesota got out their boats and fishing poles. They thanked Paul so loudly that Babe heard them and came home to Paul.

Vocabulary Skills

Circle the word in each pair that has a short vowel sound like the sound in *tip* or *jam*.

1. state   sad

2. pin   pine

3. made   mad

4. hill   hole

5. bat   boat

Write the story words that have these meanings.

6. mad

_____
(Par. 1)

7. went up

_____
(Par. 1)

Reading Skills

1. How did Paul solve the problem with the holes?

_____

_____

_____

2. Why did Babe run away?

_____

_____

3. What made Babe come back?

_____

_____

4. People who tell tall tales stretch the truth. List one idea from the story that can't be true.

_____

_____

_____

Afternoon Art

Read to see what Mom and Matt draw.

1 "May I have the green, please?" asked Matt.

2 "Sure," said Mom. She handed it over. "Are you making more trees?"

3 "No," said Matt, "I'm done with trees. I'm drawing a turtle now. What are you working on?"

4 Mom held up her paper. A big orange flower filled the page. Matt smiled. "That's the flower in Gram's garden, isn't it?"

5 "That's what I'm trying to make it look like," said Mom. "Drawing pretty flowers helps me remember them when the flowers are all gone."

6 Matt nodded. "And drawing this turtle helps me remember the one we saw by the road last week."

7 "May I have the orange, please?" asked Mom.

8 "More flowers?" Matt asked.

9 "No. Cheese," teased Mom. "I'm trying to remember my lunch. I'm hungry."

Vocabulary Skills

Circle the best word for each sentence. Then, write it in the blank.

1. Matt uses _____ for his turtle.

   blue   green   brown

2. Mom wants to remember Gram's _____.

   flowers   cheese   trees

3. Matt and Mom enjoy _____.

   brushes   drawing   train

Each of these words has an ending. Underline the base words.

4. handed

5. drawing

6. trees

7. trying

8. helps

9. working

10. filled

Reading Skills

1. This story is mostly about

   _____ how to draw.

   _____ Matt and Mom drawing.

   _____ choosing colors.

Words such as *he, she, I, this,* and *them* take the place of other words. Read these story sentences. Then, fill in the blanks.

2. "May I have the green, please?" asked Matt.

   I stands for _____.

3. "Sure," said Mom. She handed it over.

   She stands for _____.

4. "Drawing pretty flowers helps me remember them when the flowers are all gone."

   Them stands for _____.

Circle the best answer.

5. What do you think Mom and Matt will do next?

   get ready for bed

   go to school

   have a snack

What Is an Art Museum?

Read to find out what an art museum is.

1 Art comes in all sizes and shapes. It might be pretty, or it might be unusual. If you look for it, you can see art all around you. It might be a building, a picture on a poster, or a shape in the sand.

2 A place where people take care of art so that other people can see it is called an *art museum.* Some museums take care of art that is very old. Old art helps us learn about the people who made it long, long ago.

3 Some museums take care of new art. New art helps us see the world in different ways. It might make us ask questions, or it might make us laugh.

4 Most big cities have art museums. Some are big and famous. Others are small and not famous. All of them take good care of their art, though, so that people can see it and learn about it.

Vocabulary Skills

Put a check mark by the meaning that fits the underlined word in each sentence.

1. It might be a building, a picture on a poster, or a shape in the <u>sand</u>.

   _____ tiny bits of dirt

   _____ to make wood smooth

2. It <u>might</u> make us ask questions, or it might make us laugh.

   _____ strength

   _____ maybe

Circle the word in each pair that has a long vowel sound like the sound in *case* or *fine*.

3. simple   size

4. shape   sharp

5. past   place

6. take   tack

Reading Skills

Look at each picture and circle the sentence that goes with it.

1. The blue vase is broken.

   The vase is round and tall.

2. Sue was unhappy with her picture.

   Sue's picture shows a house.

3. What can we learn from old art?

   _____

   _____

4. Tell in your own words what an art museum is.

   _____

   _____

Animal Shelter News

What is Carly excited about?

1 Carly's fork dropped against her plate. She felt her face turn red. Her dad had invited a friend from work for dinner. Mr. Mendez was right next to Carly. She felt a little nervous.

2 "Mrs. Blake," said Mr. Mendez, "thank you for such a fine meal. I do wish my wife had been able to come."

3 "You're welcome, and so do we," Mrs. Blake smiled. "Did you say there was a problem at work?"

4 "Yes," said Mr. Mendez, shaking his head. "She has been working extra hours. The animal shelter is so busy in spring."

5 "Why is it so busy?" Carly asked.

6 Mr. Mendez looked down at Carly. "This is the time of year when many kittens are born."

7 "Kittens!" said Carly so loudly that her face turned red again. "Did you hear that, Mom?"

NAME _____

Vocabulary Skills

Write the story words that have these meanings.

1. uneasy, upset

_____
(Par. 1)

2. a married woman

_____
(Par. 2)

3. trouble

_____
(Par. 3)

4. twelve months

_____
(Par. 6)

Circle the three words in each line that belong together.

5. plate   fork   meal   rug

6. wife   clerk   sister   uncle

7. red   said   cried   called

8. chick   dog   kitten   puppy

9. spring   yes   summer   winter

Reading Skills

1. Why does Carly's face turn red the first time?

_____

_____

2. Why couldn't Mrs. Mendez come to dinner?

_____

_____

3. Why does Carly's face turn red the second time?

_____

_____

Circle the best answer.

4. What do you think will happen next?

Mrs. Mendez will arrive.

Carly will ask for a kitten.

Carly's cat will enter the room.

The Case for a Cat

What does Carly's family talk about after dinner?

1 "Did you hear what Mr. Mendez said about the animal shelter?" Carly asked. "They have *too many kittens*!"

2 Mom was washing dishes. She didn't turn around. "Yes, it's sad that so many animals don't have homes."

3 "We could give one a home!" said Carly. Now, Mom turned around, shaking her head.

4 "Dad and I would like you to have a pet," explained Mom, "but our apartment is so small."

5 "The Hamlins live just two apartments down. They have a cat," objected Carly.

6 Mom frowned. She looked at Dad. "Dad and I will have to talk about it," she said slowly. "We need to think hard about whether we are ready for a cat or not."

7 "Okay," said Carly. Then, she grinned. "If you need any help, let me know. I'll help you think."

Vocabulary Skills

Circle the best word for each sentence. Then, write it in the blank.

1. A pet needs a good

_____.

roam   home   fame

2. Carly really wants a

_____.

pet   meat   boat

3. Mom will _____ the dishes.

cash   wash   fish

4. Dad will _____ the dishes.

dry   why   cry

The missing word in each sentence sounds like *head*. Change the first letter in *head* to **br, l,** or **thr.** Fill in the blanks.

5. I love the smell of fresh

_____.

6. My spool of _____ is empty.

7. I just broke my pencil

_____.

Reading Skills

1. This story is mostly about

_____ cats and dogs as pets.

_____ a girl who wants a kitten.

_____ doing chores at home.

2. Carly thinks getting a cat is a good idea. What reasons does she give?

_____

_____

_____

3. What reason does Mom give for not getting a pet?

_____

_____

4. What would you do if you were Carly?

_____

_____

_____

Cats Long Ago

Read to learn part of the history of cats.

1   Imagine that it is three thousand years ago. You are visiting Egypt. You see a statue of a cat. You go into a building and there are cats everywhere! People are feeding them and taking care of them. Everyone seems to like cats.

2   "Why so many cats?" you wonder. To answer that question, we have to learn a little bit about Egypt.

3   The Egyptians grew grain for food and to trade with other people. They stored their grain in huge buildings. Rats and mice, in particular, also liked to eat grain. Cats, which eat rats and mice, were the best way to protect the grain.

4   Cats became the most respected animal in Egypt. When a family's cat died, the family members shaved their eyebrows to show that a sad and important thing had happened.

NAME _____

Vocabulary Skills

Read each sentence and circle the word that is made of two shorter words. Write the two words on the lines.

1. I saw cats everywhere!

   _____ _____

2. Everyone showed respect for them.

   _____ _____

3. They would shave their eyebrows.

   _____ _____

Circle the best word for each sentence. Then, write the word in the blank.

4. In Egypt, people took _____ care of cats.

   good   goof   goal

5. They stored _____ in huge buildings.

   grain   grim   great

6. The cats took care of the _____ and mice.

   real   rain   rats

Reading Skills

1. The author wrote "Cats Long Ago" mostly to

   _____ give information.

   _____ make you laugh.

2. Compare what you know about cats in Egypt with what you know about cats today. One idea is written for you.

   In Egypt

   <u>cats were respected</u>

   _____

   _____

   Today

   <u>cats are usually well cared for</u>

   _____

   _____

3. What is one difference between us and the people in Egypt long ago?

   _____

   _____

Spectrum Reading Grade 2

31

Cats Every Day

What kind of care does a cat need?

1   Like all house pets, cats need food, water, and a certain amount of attention every day.

Food

2   A cat needs its food dish filled every day. A box of cat food costs several dollars. An adult cat may eat a box in less than two weeks.

Water

3   A cat needs to have fresh water each day. You will probably have to fill the dish twice a day.

Other Needs

4   If a cat lives indoors, it needs a litter box. Cat litter costs several dollars for a 10-pound bag. The bag lasts for several weeks. The litter box, however, should be cleaned out almost every day.

5   Once a cat becomes your pet, it will depend on you for almost all of its needs. Are you ready?

Vocabulary Skills

Find a word in the story whose meaning is the same as these words.

1. grown up

_____
(Par. 2)

2. new, not stale

_____
(Par. 3)

3. in a house

_____
(Par. 4)

4. nearly

_____
(Par. 4)

Add **s** at the end of a word to show that there is more than one. Write these words so that they mean more than one.

5. cat _____

6. day _____

7. week _____

8. pet _____

Reading Skills

1. This article is mostly about

_____ cats in animal shelters.

_____ how cute kittens are.

_____ daily cat care.

2. After reading the article, do you think you could care for a cat? Why or why not?

_____

_____

Study Skills

1. Write one idea that you find under each heading.

Food

_____

Water

_____

Other Needs

_____

2. Why do you think the author used headings in this article?

_____

Comb the Cat, Please!

What does a cat need besides food and water?

Grooming

1   Cats are very clean animals. They use their rough tongues to bathe themselves several times a day. Sometimes they like help, though. To keep a cat's coat in shape, it is a good idea to comb or brush the cat once or twice a week. If you have a long-haired cat, you may need to brush it every day to keep its fur neat.

Health Care

2   All kittens should visit a vet and get several shots. These shots help prevent common cat illnesses. An adult cat should visit a vet once a year for a check-up and to get booster shots.

3   Unless your family plans to breed and raise cats, your cat should have an operation so that it cannot have kittens. This prevents unwanted kittens from ending up stray or at the animal shelter.

Vocabulary Skills

The missing words in these sentences contain the letters **oa**. Fill in the blanks.

1. Brush a cat's _____ to keep it shiny.

2. Under the chin is the _____.

3. For a bath, use mild _____.

Read these words and look at the pictures.

the cat's bed   Tasha's cat

Add **'s** to show that something belongs to something else or someone. Show that these pets belong to their owners.

4. Mel has a cat.

   It is Mel_____ cat.

5. Cal has a rabbit.

   It is Cal_____ rabbit.

6. Shawna has a dog.

   It is Shawna_____ dog.

Reading Skills

1. What do cats do for themselves?

   _____

   _____

2. What should a cat owner do once a year?

   _____

   _____

3. Why might a long-haired cat need to be brushed more often than a short-haired cat?

   _____

   _____

4. If you had a cat, would you rather have a short-haired cat or a long-haired cat? Write why.

   _____

   _____

Cat or No Cat?

Will Carly's hopes go up or down?

1   "Carly, would you and Mitch come here, please? We want to talk to you about something," Dad called from the kitchen.

2   "Coming, Dad," said Carly. To her little brother, she said, "Come on, Mitch. Maybe this is about a kitten!"

3   Mom and Dad were sitting at the kitchen table. They looked thoughtful. Carly and Mitch sat down. Dad spoke first. Carly's hopes sank. Dad always gave out the bad news. "Your mother and I have been talking about a cat." Carly held on to a tiny bit of hope.

4   Then, Mom spoke up. Carly's hopes perked up a little higher. "We don't think a kitten is a good idea." *Boom!* Carly's hopes landed on the ground.

5   Mom went on, "We think it would be better if we got a grown-up cat."

Vocabulary Skills

Circle the best word for each sentence. Then, write it in the blank.

1. Carly has high _____.

   hello   hill   hopes

2. Carly _____ her dad will say "no."

   thinks   then   throw

3. Mitch also _____ to have a cat.

   went   woke   wants

The missing word in each sentence sounds like *kite*. Change the **k** in *kite* to **b**, **wh**, or **wr**. Fill in the blanks.

4. An unfriendly cat might _____.

5. I will _____ and tell you about my cat.

6. Snowball is a _____ cat, of course.

Study Skills

Write each set of words in A-B-C order.

1. something   kitchen   please

   _____

   _____

   _____

2. table   news   first

   _____

   _____

   _____

3. higher   kitten   idea

   _____

   _____

   _____

Choose a Cat

Which cat will Carly and Mitch choose?

1 "It's our first pet, so we would like to start with a grown-up cat," explained Mom.

2 Mrs. Mendez smiled. "I think that's a smart idea for a first pet. It's a little easier. Feel free to look around. Just wave if you have questions," said Mrs. Mendez as she turned away.

3 Carly and Mitch were already looking around. An orange tiger cat looked at Mitch, but then it walked away. Carly saw a big black cat. She held out her hand. The cat hissed and batted at her hand.

4 "You are not very friendly!" cried Carly, pulling her hand back. Just then, a gray cat with white paws rubbed against Carly's ankles, then against Mitch's.

5 Mitch smiled at Carly. "This one has picked us, Carly."

Vocabulary Skills

Write the story words that have these meanings.

1. animal kept at home

   _____
   (Par. 1)

2. less hard

   _____
   (Par. 2)

3. made a snake-like sound

   _____
   (Par. 3)

4. brushed against

   _____
   (Par. 4)

Put a check mark by the meaning that fits the underlined word in each sentence.

5. One <u>wave</u> soaked me to the skin.

   _____ to move the hand back and forth

   _____ movement on the surface of a lake or ocean

6. For lunch today, I had an <u>orange</u>.

   _____ a fruit

   _____ a color

Reading Skills

1. This story is mostly about

   _____ choosing a cat.

   _____ Mr. Mendez's work.

   _____ kittens who need homes.

2. Why didn't Carly choose the big black cat?

   _____

   _____

   _____

3. How did Mitch and Carly choose the gray cat?

   _____

   _____

   _____

Mouse in the House

Read about Mouse's first day in his new home.

1   Carly opened her eyes and stretched. What was special about today?

2   "Oh," she cried, throwing back the covers. "Mouse! Where are you? Here, kitty, kitty, kitty!"

3   It had been easy to pick a name for the new cat. He was gray, and he made a tiny little mewing sound. "Mouse" was perfect. But where was he now? Carly looked under her bed. Mitch looked, too.

4   Carly passed through the kitchen. "Mom, have you seen Mouse?"

5   "Not since I gave him his breakfast," she said over the newspaper. "Did you try the living room?"

6   On the living room floor was a big patch of sunshine. Right in the middle was Mouse. He was curled up and sound asleep.

7   Mouse was at home.

Vocabulary Skills

Read each sentence and circle the word that is made of two shorter words. Write the two words on the lines.

1. Mom was reading the newspaper.

   _____   _____

2. Mouse liked the warm sunshine.

   _____   _____

Circle the best word for each sentence. Then, write it in the blank.

3. Carly knew today was _____.

   space   special   speed

4. She found Mouse _____ in the sun.

   sleeping   sliding   slipping

5. Carly was quiet so she wouldn't _____ the cat.

   scarf   score   scare

Reading Skills

1. Which sentence best tells how Carly feels about today?

   _____ She is excited.

   _____ She is worried.

2. What words or ideas in the story helped you answer question 1?

   _____

   _____

3. Where did Carly and Mitch look first for Mouse?

   _____

4. In what room did Carly find Mouse?

   _____

5. Why was Mouse sleeping there?

   _____

   _____

   _____

A Letter From Kyle

What news does Kyle send to his grandparents?

Dear Grandma and Grandpa,

1   How are you? I am fine. School is out already. On our last day, we had a picnic out on the baseball field. It was fun until we all had to dash out of the rain. Even that was kind of fun, though.

2   How was your camping trip? Dad says you're just getting back home today. We took good care of Sparky for you. He sleeps at the foot of my bed on most nights. He and the cat have even been getting along. I think Snowy must have had a talk with Sparky. When Snowy walks into the room, Sparky leaves!

3   Dad says to tell you that our garden is looking good this year. We've had lots of rain, especially on that last day of school.

4   When are you coming to get Sparky? See you soon.

Love,
Kyle

Vocabulary Skills

Each of these words has an ending. Underline the base words.

1. camping

2. says

3. sleeps

4. getting

5. leaves

Write the shorter word from the box that stands for the underlined words in each sentence.

I'll	we've
you're	

6. Does Dad know when <u>you are</u> leaving?

_____

7. After <u>we have</u> had lunch, we will walk Sparky.

_____

8. Later, <u>I will</u> write a letter.

_____

Reading Skills

1. Why was there a picnic on the baseball field?

_____

_____

2. Why did everyone have to dash into the school?

_____

_____

3. Why is Kyle's family taking care of Sparky?

_____

_____

4. Why does Sparky leave the room when Snowy comes in?

_____

_____

Kyle Gets Mail

What did Kyle's grandparents see on their camping trip?

Dear Kyle,

1   Our camping trip was wonderful! We're already talking about going to the same place next year. There is so much to see. I think you and your parents would like it, too.

2   From Ohio, we drove south to Kentucky. We enjoy looking at rocks, so we had decided to go to Mammoth Cave State Park. We made the right choice! I've never seen so many rocks!

3   Each day, we chose a different cave. We saw narrow places and huge, high rooms. In one cave, we were underground for more than two miles.

4   We'll come to get Sparky next weekend, if that's okay. We hope he hasn't been unhappy.

Love,
Grandma and Grandpa

Vocabulary Skills

Circle the best word for each sentence. Then, write it in the blank.

1. Kyle's grandparents were happy with their _____.

   choice   check   chart

2. How _____ those rock walls must be!

   third   thick   thing

3. Through some caves, a _____ flows.

   spring   strong   swing

The prefix **un**- means *not*. Add **un** to the beginning of these words to complete these sentences.

4. Kyle was _____able to find Sparky.

5. Kyle hoped Sparky wasn't _____happy.

6. Snowy scratched Sparky, but Sparky was _____hurt.

Reading Skills

1. Where did Kyle's grandparents go on their trip?

   _____

   _____

2. Why did they go there?

   _____

   _____

3. What did you learn about Kyle's grandparents by reading their letter?

   _____

   _____

   _____

   _____

Mammoth Cave, Kentucky

What would you like to see at Mammoth Cave?

1   For natural beauty, there is no spot quite like Mammoth Cave National Park. Beneath the park lies the longest cave system on earth. There are more than 350 miles of underground passages. That's more than three times longer than any other cave we know about. Some scientists think that there are hundreds of miles yet to be found!

2   If you go, you can follow a path that humans walked on four thousand years ago. You can see crystals that are millions of years old. If you're lucky, you might see an eyeless fish.

3   Though the cave passages are dark, more than 200 kinds of animals live in them. Many of these use the cave only part of the time. Some, however, can live only in the dark, cool cave.

Vocabulary Skills

Put each word in the right blank.

beneath	**cave**
underground	

1. One _____ passage is very steep.

2. A huge room in the cave is _____ a hill.

3. We know that humans were in the _____ long, long ago.

Put a check mark by the meaning that fits the underlined word in each sentence.

4. We camped in a beautiful <u>spot</u>.

_____ a place

_____ a stain

5. Many people <u>fish</u> in Kentucky's lakes.

_____ to try to catch with bait

_____ an animal that lives in water

Reading Skills

1. This article is mostly about

_____ how caves are formed.

_____ the sights in Mammoth Cave.

_____ animals that live in caves.

2. What is special about Mammoth Cave?

_____

_____

3. Why might a fish that lives in a cave not have any eyes?

_____

_____

4. If you went to Mammoth Cave, what would you most like to see? Write why.

_____

_____

_____

Post by Post

What is hard about painting a fence?

1   "Is this everything we need, Dad?" Michelle looked at her dad in his painting hat. It was covered with so much paint that you couldn't see the words anymore.

2   Dad looked grim. "No. We need a radio. I can't paint without some good painting music."

3   "I'll get the old one from the basement," Michelle called out as she ran into the house. When she got back, Dad had stirred the paint. Now, he was staring at the fence. It went all the way around the yard.

4   "On each post," Dad explained, "you have to do the front, then both side edges."

5   "The front, the edge, and the other edge," repeated Michelle. She made a little song out of it. Then, she sang it so many times she thought she would blow up. And there were still 472 posts to go!

Vocabulary Skills

Circle the word in each pair that has a long vowel sound like the sound in *post* or *side*.

1. old   got

2. grim   times

3. blow   not

4. still   while

Write these words so that they mean more than one.

5. post _____

6. house _____

7. fence _____

8. edge _____

9. song _____

Reading Skills

1. Write **1**, **2**, and **3** by these sentences to show what happened first, next, and last.

    _____ Dad stirred the paint.

    _____ Michelle got the radio.

    _____ Dad and Michelle painted.

2. What does Michelle have to do on each post?

    _____

    _____

3. Why does Michelle think she will blow up?

    _____

    _____

4. Have you ever done a task that went on and on and on? Write about it.

    _____

    _____

    _____

Mixed-Up Day

What goes wrong for Danny?

1   It all started at breakfast. The milk jumped out of the jug and flowed all over the table and all over me. I barely had time to clean up the table and put on a clean shirt.

2   On the way to school, I saw myself in a store window. Bed head! My hair was sticking up to the sky on one side, and the shirt I had on did not match my pants.

3   At school, I headed right to the water fountain so I could wet down my hair. I pushed the button. Nothing happened. I pushed again and looked closely to see what was wrong. All of a sudden, the water spurted up into my face. My hair was fixed, sort of, but now my shirt was soaked.

4   I slid into my desk, hoping no one would notice. Mr. Torres looked right at me. "Oh, Danny. Tomorrow is Mix-Up Day, not today."

Vocabulary Skills

Write the story words that have the same meanings as these words.

1. container

_____
(Par. 1)

2. dampen

_____
(Par. 3)

3. incorrect

_____
(Par. 3)

4. saw

_____
(Par. 4)

In each row, circle the two words with opposite meanings.

5. jump   clean   dirty   help

6. left   pants   sticking   right

7. wet   push   looked   dry

8. closely   spurted   fixed   broken

Reading Skills

Put each word in the right blank.

water	hair	milk

1. First, Danny spilled the

_____.

2. Then, he had a problem with

his _____.

3. Next, he got sprayed with

_____.

4. What did Danny look like when he sat down in his desk?

_____

_____

5. Have you ever had a mixed-up day? Write about it.

_____

_____

_____

_____

Mountain Magic

How does the girls' project turn out?

1 "Oh, we missed a spot," said Hailey, pointing.

2 "Okay," said Megan, dabbing at the spot. "Are we done now?" She and her best friend, Hailey, had made a volcano out of wet, sticky goop. They were painting it to look like a mountain.

3 The next day, they were ready for fun. Megan thought out loud, "Mrs. Metzer said the baking soda goes first, then the vinegar. Right?"

4 "That's right," said Megan's mom. "Are you ready for the lava?"

5 "Ready!" they said together.

6 In went the baking soda. The girls held their breath. In went the vinegar. It hit the soda and bubbled up, up, up, and over the edge of the volcano.

7 Megan and Hailey clapped. "Yea, it worked! Let's do it again!"

Vocabulary Skills

Write the story words that have these meanings.

1. touching lightly

_____
(Par. 2)

2. a mass of land that rises above the nearby area

_____
(Par. 2)

3. rim

_____
(Par. 6)

Circle the letters that complete each word. Then, write the letters in the blank.

4. Megan and Hailey were ready to st_____t.

ir   ar   or

5. The baking soda went in f_____st.

er   ur   ir

Reading Skills

1. Write **1**, **2**, **3**, and **4** by these sentences to show what happened first, second, third, and last.

_____ The girls painted the volcano.

_____ The friends made a volcano.

_____ Bubbles came up out of the volcano.

_____ Baking soda and vinegar went into the volcano.

Some of these sentences are about **real** things. Write **R** by them. The other sentences are about **make-believe** things. Write **M** by them.

2. _____ The girls can build a real volcano.

3. _____ A real volcano can be on someone's back porch.

4. _____ The girls do projects together.

5. _____ Mothers help with projects.

Spectrum Reading Grade 2

53

Making Plans

Read to see what the Shaws are planning.

1   "Where will they sleep?" Lisa asked her mom. Lisa was wondering if she could fit two cousins in her bed without hurting any stuffed animals.

2   "They'll sleep in the green bedroom, just like last time," answered Mrs. Shaw.

3   Lisa was a little bit glad. "Oh, that's good," she said. Now, she had another question. "What will they do?" Lisa was wondering if she had enough dress-up clothes to go around.

4   "I'm not sure yet. They'll be here for a week. We'll have to plan some things," said Mrs. Shaw. "I thought we might spend one day at the zoo."

5   "I vote for the zoo, too," Lisa replied.

Vocabulary Skills

A word part that makes one sound is a **syllable**. The word *but* has one syllable. The word *button* has two syllables. Words, like *button* or *melted*, that have two consonants between two vowels, are divided between the consonants: *but / ton*, *mel / ted*. Draw a line to divide each word below into syllables.

I. j u m p e r

2. u n t i l

3. f o l l o w

4. b a t t e r

5. p e r s o n

6. o r d e r

The missing word in each sentence sounds like *sheet*. Change the **sh** in *sheet* to **f** or **gr**. Fill in the blanks.

7. Lisa was happy to
_____ her cousins.

8. Mom asked us to wipe our
_____.

Reading Skills

Look at each picture and circle the sentence that goes with it.

I. Lisa's bed is neat.

Lisa's bed is empty.

2. Lisa's dress is too big.

Lisa's dress is short.

What do you think will happen next? Circle the correct answer.

3. Lisa and her brother will go to bed.

The cousins will arrive soon.

Lisa will hide her dress-up clothes.

To the Zoo

What would you want to see at the zoo?

1   "Is everyone buckled in?" called Mrs. Shaw.

2   "Yes, Mom. Hold on, tigers. Here I come!" sang Jake from the back seat.

3   "Ooh, tigers? You didn't tell me there were tigers there," said Charlie. "Here we come!"

4   Julia was very grown-up. "I would rather spend my time looking at animals that don't want to eat me. I like to watch the owls."

5   "An owl would eat you if you were a mouse!" called Charlie. Julia made a face.

6   "What about you, Lisa?" Mrs. Shaw asked. "What do you want to see?"

7   "Make mine zebras," she answered, after thinking for a moment.

8   Mrs. Shaw laughed. "Zebras, tigers, and owls—oh, my!"

Vocabulary Skills

Put a check mark by the meaning that fits the underlined word in each sentence.

1. Let Mom <u>watch</u> the road.

_____ see, look at

_____ a machine that keeps time

2. This car seat is <u>mine</u>.

_____ a place for digging rocks

_____ belongs to me

Circle the word in each pair that has a short vowel sound like the sound in *men*.

3.   yes   seat

4.   tear   tell

5.   spend   eat

Reading Skills

1. How does everyone feel about going to the zoo?

_____ They are tired.

_____ They are eager.

Words such as *he*, *she*, and *I* take the place of other words. Read these story sentences. Then, fill in the blanks.

2. "Here I come!" sang Jake from the back seat.

I stands for _____

3. Julia was very grown-up. "I would rather spend my time looking at animals that don't want to eat me."

Me stands for _____

4. "What about you, Lisa?" Mrs. Shaw asked.

You stands for _____

Write each word in the correct blank.

buckled   spend

5. The car doesn't go until everyone is _____ in.

6. Watch how much you _____ at the zoo.

7. What animals would you like to see if you went to the zoo?

_____

_____

_____

Zebra News

Read to learn about zebras.

Where Zebras Live

[1] Wild zebras live only in Africa. They choose open country that has some areas of trees and grass.

How Zebras Live

[2] Zebras move together in large groups called *herds*. They often travel with herds of other animals, such as antelopes, wildebeest, and gnus. Zebras graze, or eat grass. When the grass is gone in one area, the herd moves to another area.

Other Zebra News

[3] How can you tell one zebra from another? By their stripes, of course. Each zebra's stripes are different from every other zebra's stripes. The animals' stripes help them blend together when they are in a herd. That makes it harder for lions to single out and catch one zebra.

Vocabulary Skills

Look at these words. They are broken into syllables. Sound out each syllable. Then, say the words aloud.

1. antelopes
   an / te / lopes

2. wildebeest
   wil / de / beest

The missing words in these sentences contain the letters **oi**. Fill in the blanks.

3. If the herd is running, you will hear the _____.

4. If I had a _____, I would watch the otters.

5. I hope the rain doesn't _____ our trip.

Reading Skills

1. What is a large group of zebras called?

   _____

2. Why does a herd move from place to place?

   _____

   _____

3. What are some other animals that move in groups?

   _____

   _____

4. Why do zebras' stripes make it hard for lions to catch a zebra?

   _____

   _____

   _____

Tiger Tips

Read to learn something new about tigers.

Where Tigers Live

¹ You might find a tiger on a mountain, in a deep forest, or in a wet, grassy area. You will have to go to Asia, however, to find one in the wild.

How Tigers Live

² If you're looking for a tiger in the middle of the day, look in cool places. Tigers stay out of the heat by sleeping in caves or by lying in thick grass or in shallow water. After a day of rest, the tiger is ready to hunt all night. Once a tiger catches its meal, it drags it to a quiet place to eat in peace.

Other Tiger Tips

³ If you're looking for a tiger cub, look for its mother. A mother tiger, or *tigress*, takes care of her cubs for more than two years. She protects them, brings them food, and teaches them how to hunt.

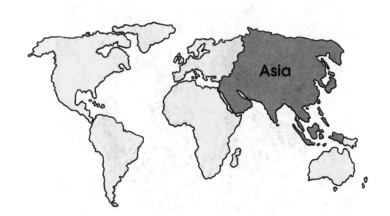

Vocabulary Skills

Circle the three words in each line that belong together.

1. river   forest   lake   pond

2. rock   grass   tree   bush

3. mountain   hill   swamp   cliff

Circle the best word for each sentence. Then, write it in the blank.

4. The lion is known as the
_____ of the beasts.

cling   king   thing

5. You may have to
_____ all day to find
a lion.

search   touch   pitch

6. A cub stays with its
_____ for more than
two years.

mother   father   brother

Reading Skills

1. In what three kinds of places do tigers live?

_____

_____

_____

2. How are these places different?

_____

_____

_____

3. How does the author help you with the word *tigress*?

_____

_____

Study Skills

1. Under what heading can you find information about when a tiger hunts?

_____

_____

Only Owls

Read to find out about owls.

Feathers

[1] Owls fly on silent wings. Their feathers are so soft that they make no noise during flight. How does that help an owl? It allows the owl to sneak up on its prey, or the animals it hunts and eats, such as mice, rats, rabbits, small birds, and insects.

Eyes and Ears

[2] Does an owl see well with its large round eyes? Yes, especially at night. Owls also have excellent hearing. In fact, they use their hearing, rather than sight, to find their prey.

Feet

[3] Why might a bird's feet be important? Owls have strong three-toed feet with sharp claws. To hunt, owls swoop down and catch their prey with their feet. Most owls then swallow their prey whole.

Vocabulary Skills

Some words change form when they are made plural. Draw a line from the singular form in the first column to the correct plural form in the second column.

1. one wing   two feet

2. one mouse   two wings

3. one foot   three toes

4. one toe   many mice

Write the story words that have these meanings.

5. quiet

_____
(Par. 1)

6. very, very good

_____
(Par. 2)

7. having a fine point

_____
(Par. 3)

Reading Skills

Use what you know or what you just read about owls to answer these questions.

1. Would owls be able to live in a city? Explain.

_____

_____

2. What would happen if an owl made noise as it flew?

_____

_____

3. This owl is asleep.

This owl is awake.

Study Skills

1. What do the three headings have in common?

_____

_____

Remembering the Zoo

What did the children like about the zoo?

1 "I wish I could sleep just like that big, old tiger," said Charlie. They had had a great day at the zoo, but he sure was tired. He remembered the tigers and smiled though.

2 "He was lying in the dirt," said Julia, making a face. "I would like to be up on a high branch. That's where wise animals sleep." She thought of the owls and smiled.

3 Jake was still ready for action. "Not me," he spoke up. "I'm glad one of the tigers was awake. I wish I could climb rocks like he did." Everyone nodded, thinking about the strong animal and how easily he had moved.

4 After a long time, Lisa had a question. "Mom?" she asked in a small voice. "Do you think I would look good in stripes?"

Vocabulary Skills

Circle the best word for each sentence. Then, write it in the blank.

1. Charlie wanted to
_____.

    smart   hear   rest

2. Julia wanted to _____ in a tree.

    sleep   mop   trap

3. Jake is still ready for
_____.

    spin   noon   action

4. Lisa was _____ to ask her question.

    shed   afraid   blend

In each row, circle the two words with opposite meanings.

5. awake   wise   foolish   dirty

6. weak   action   strong   tired

Reading Skills

1. Why didn't Julia care for the sleeping tiger?

    _____

    _____

2. Why does Lisa want stripes?

    _____

    _____

Some of these sentences are about **real** things. Write **R** by them. The other sentences are about **make-believe** things. Write **M** by them.

3. _____ Animals ride in car seats.

4. _____ Children sleep in beds.

5. _____ People climb rocks.

6. _____ Girls perch in trees.

Waving Good-Bye

What does the boy remember about his grandparents' visit?

1 I stood on the porch for a long time and waved. Gram and Gramps had such a long drive. They wouldn't get home until tomorrow.

2 Everything seemed quiet now that they were gone. Gramps wasn't telling one of his stories. The best one was about the fort he and his brothers had built in the hay barn. It seemed as if the fort got bigger every time I heard the story.

3 And Gram wasn't in the kitchen humming like she always did. Every now and then, she would even dance a little. Then, she'd look up and laugh. If anyone was watching, her face would turn red.

4 I watched until their car was just a dot. Then, I hummed a little song and went to ask my dad about the hay in the barn.

Vocabulary Skills

Write the shorter word from the box that stands for the underlined words in each sentence.

she'd	wasn't	wouldn't

1. Gram <u>was not</u> humming in the kitchen.

   _____

2. If I caught her dancing, <u>she would</u> turn red.

   _____

3. Gramps <u>would not</u> stop telling stories.

   _____

Each of these words has an ending. Underline the base words.

4. waved

5. brothers

6. seemed

7. watched

Reading Skills

1. Which word best describes the boy's feelings about his grandparents?

   fond   excited   hopeless

2. Why do you think the fort "got bigger" every time Gramps told the story?

   _____

   _____

3. What do you think the boy might do next?

   _____

   _____

4. Mark the sentence that is true.

   _____ Gramps grew up on a farm.

   _____ Gramps grew up in the city.

5. What information in the story helped you answer question 4?

   _____

   _____

Games for a Rainy Day

What do Gina and her mom do on a rainy day?

1   *Rumble, rumble, rumble.* The afternoon thunder told me that we would not get to go swimming this afternoon. I went looking for my mom just as the first raindrops fell.

2   "What can I do, Mom?"

3   Mom looked up from her book. I saw her eyes move to the window, then she frowned. "Hmm," she said, "this looks like a day for the game closet, Gina. How about pick-up sticks? Or hopscotch?"

4   I groaned. Those were little-kid games. "Uh, anything else?" I asked hopefully.

5   Mom shook her head. "Those are good games. Let's try them." We headed for the closet.

6   Mom and I played all afternoon. Once we laughed until we fell over. It was pretty fun, even if they were little-kid games.

Vocabulary Skills

Read each sentence and circle the word that is made of two shorter words. Write the two words on the lines.

1. Gina and Mom filled a rainy afternoon.

   _____ _____

2. The raindrops told Gina that swimming was out.

   _____ _____

3. Was there anything besides kid games?

   _____ _____

Circle the word in each pair that has a short vowel sound like the sounds in *fun* and *kid*.

4. clue   rumble

5. sticks   slide

6. swim   bite

Reading Skills

1. Gina knows she will not be able to swim this afternoon because _____.

2. Mom frowned because

   _____.

3. This story is mostly about

   _____ the rules for playing hopscotch.

   _____ cleaning out a closet full of games.

   _____ how a girl and her mom spend an afternoon.

4. Why didn't Gina like her mom's ideas at first?

   _____

   _____

5. How did the afternoon turn out for Gina?

   _____

   _____

Clouds and Rain Today

Read to find out why it rains.

[1] Water is all around us—in lakes, rivers, streams, oceans, and even puddles. Heat from the sun causes tiny parts of that water to rise into the air. Those tiny parts are called *water vapor.*

[2] Up in the air, the water vapor forms clouds. The tiny parts of water in the vapor join to form small drops of water in the clouds. These drops may freeze as the clouds rise. The higher they go, the colder the air becomes.

[3] When the water drops in the cloud get too heavy, they fall back to the ground. The water falls as rain, snow, hail, or sleet. Some of the water flows back into rivers, streams, and the ocean. The next time the sun shines, the cycle starts all over again.

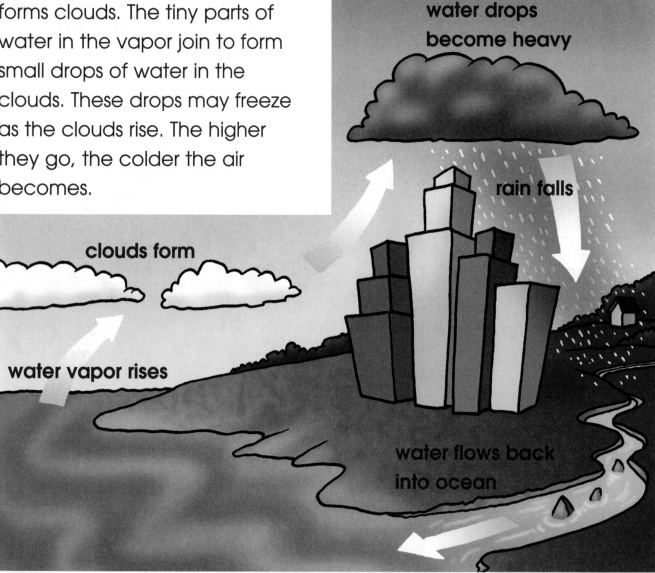

water drops become heavy

rain falls

clouds form

water vapor rises

water flows back into ocean

Vocabulary Skills

In each row, circle the letters in each word that make the same sound you hear in the underlined word.

h(ea)t tr(ee) sh(e) l(ea)f

1. <u>rain</u>   paper   wait   today

2. <u>snow</u>   road   drove   echo

3. <u>cloud</u>   out   brown   how

Write the story words that have the same meanings as these words.

4. warmth _____ (Par. 1)

5. go up _____ (Par. 2)

6. comes down _____ (Par. 3)

Reading Skills

1. Write 1, 2, 3, and 4 by these sentences to show the correct order of the steps in the water cycle.

_____ Rain, snow, hail, or sleet falls to the ground.

_____ Water vapor rises and forms clouds.

_____ The sun's heat causes water to form water vapor.

_____ Water drops form and become heavy.

Study Skills

1. Look at the picture of the water cycle. What do the arrows above the ocean tell you?

_____

_____

2. Explain the water cycle in your own words.

_____

_____

_____

_____

Shopping With Dad

What does Gina learn at the store?

1   I like shopping with my dad. The other day, we went to the grocery store. I laughed so hard I almost fell over. I learned something, too. It all started when Dad got excited about the corn on the cob.

2   "What's the big deal? There is fresh food here all the time," I said.

3   "Yes, that's true, Gina," agreed Dad, "but it's nice to see fresh food that was grown nearby. Then, we know it's really fresh."

4   "Oh," I said. I guess Dad could tell I didn't get it. He explained.

5   "Some of the fresh food was picked many days ago, maybe even weeks ago. Then, it probably got washed, put into packages, loaded onto a truck, and unloaded here."

6   "Oh," I said. We chose six ears. It was the best corn I ever ate. Now I get it.

Vocabulary Skills

The prefix **re**- means *again*. Add **re** to the beginning of these words to complete these sentences.

I. Dad had to _____write the list.

2. Gina wanted to _____heat her lunch.

3. Mom had to _____wash the corn.

Put a check mark by the meaning that fits the underlined word in each sentence.

4. All I could think about was sinking my teeth into that <u>corn</u>.

_____ a vegetable

_____ a sore spot on a toe

5. I turned my <u>ear</u> in his direction.

_____ a cob of corn

_____ human organ related to hearing

Reading Skills

Put each word in the right blank.

    excited   fresh   picked

I. Dad got _____ about the corn.

2. Have you ever _____ corn?

3. Some people won't eat anything but _____ corn.

4. Why does Gina's dad get excited about the corn?

_____

_____

5. Why isn't some of the fresh food really fresh?

_____

_____

_____

Backyard Corn

Learn how to grow corn by reading the passage below.

1   Corn is fairly easy to grow. Even in a small backyard garden, a family can grow enough corn for quite a number of yummy meals.

2   First, take care of the soil, just like for any garden. Work it up as deeply as you can. Chop up clumps of dirt, and rake the surface smooth.

3   Next comes the planting. Place seeds 2 inches deep and about 12 inches apart.

Your rows should be about 2 feet apart. Keep the soil moist. You'll have to wait for 10 to 15 days for the seeds to sprout. Once they do sprout, water them (if it doesn't rain), and keep the rows clear of weeds.

4   About 70 to 90 days after you plant your corn seeds, you will be able to enjoy your first harvest. Pass the butter and the salt, please!

Vocabulary Skills

Circle the word in each pair that has a short vowel sound like the sounds in *hot* and *ran*.

1. do   chop

2. stop   row

3. pass   day

4. paint   plant

Reading Skills

Write these steps in the correct order.

- watch plants grow

- plant seeds

- water soil

- harvest corn

- prepare soil

1. _____

2. _____

3. _____

4. _____

5. _____

Study Skills

Write each set of words in A-B-C order.

1. corn   garden   backyard

_____

_____

_____

2. soil   dirt   clumps

_____

_____

_____

3. seeds   rows   weeds

_____

_____

_____

4. plant   harvest   days

_____

_____

_____

Corn: How We Use It

What are some different uses of corn?

1 There was a time when the only use for corn was to eat it or to feed it to the cattle or hogs. Those days are long gone.

2 There may be as many as four thousand products at your grocery store that contain corn. No, they're not putting corn kernels in your peanut butter. But they might be sweetening the peanut butter with corn syrup. And there may be another corn product—corn starch—in items such as baked goods and laundry soaps. If you drive home from the store, you could use a fuel made from corn called *ethanol*.

3 About half of the corn that American farmers grow is still fed to cattle and hogs. The other half, though, shows up in everything from paper to shampoo, from medicine to the glue on a postage stamp.

Vocabulary Skills

Circle the letters that complete each word. Then, write the letters in the blank.

1. Did you have c_____n last week?

   ur   er   or

2. These muffins are sweetened with corn s_____up.

   yr   ur   ar

3. Does your laundry soap contain corn st_____ch?

   ir   ar   er

The missing words in these sentences contain the letters **ou**. Fill in the blanks.

4. The news _____ the corn crop is good.

5. I can't name four hundred things, much less four _____ things made of corn!

6. Listen to the _____ of the corn blowing in the wind.

Reading Skills

1. Today, corn is used in thousands of products. How is that different from many years ago?

   _____

   _____

2. The article mentions two products that come from corn. What are they?

   _____

   _____

   What are they used for?

   _____

   _____

3. Half of the corn grown in America is fed to cattle and hogs. Why is that important?

   _____

   _____

   _____

Something New for Gina

Read to see what Gina learns at the picnic.

1 Tonight was the Nolan Street picnic. We have one every year. Everyone takes one dish of food. Then, you go along the table and you wonder what to try because some of it looks sort of unusual.

2 "Gina, don't you want some of this salad? It has raisins in it." Mom never gives up.

3 "Um, no, thanks, Mom. I took some apple slices for my salad." I took other safe things, such as potato salad and baked beans. Then, my dad came up all of a sudden.

4 "Gina, try this pizza. It is great!" he said. Before I could say anything, he popped a piece into my mouth.

5 "Hey, Dad! This isn't pizza."

6 "Ah, but it is. It's fruit pizza," he said, grinning.

7 I asked for another piece. Then, I asked Mrs. Taylor for the recipe.

Vocabulary Skills

Write the story words that have these meanings.

1. outdoor meal

_____
(Par. 1)

2. not common

_____
(Par. 1)

3. dried grapes

_____
(Par. 2)

4. smiling widely

_____
(Par. 6)

Circle the best word for each sentence. Then, write the word in the blank.

5. Gina was not eager to try the _____ at the picnic.

salt   salads   sales

6. Gina was surprised to find _____ on the pizza.

fine   faint   fruit

Reading Skills

Words such as *she*, *you*, and *it* take the place of other words. Read these story sentences. Then, fill in the blanks.

1. "Gina, don't you want some of this salad?"

You stands for _____.

2. "Gina, try this pizza. It is great!" he said.

It stands for _____.

3. Which of these sentences best tells how Gina feels about food?

_____ If it's food, I'll try it.

_____ I like to try new foods.

_____ I'll try something only if I know what it is.

_____ I like trying foods that have fruit in them.

4. Did Gina like the fruit pizza? How could you tell?

_____

_____

Fruit Pizza

Does this sound like something you would like to try?

Ingredients

- 1 package (20 ounces) sugar cookie dough

- 8 ounces cream cheese, softened

- $\frac{1}{3}$ cup sugar

- $\frac{1}{2}$ teaspoon vanilla extract

- $\frac{1}{2}$ cup orange marmalade

- 2 tablespoons water

- 4–6 types of fruit (bananas, oranges, blueberries, seedless grapes, strawberries, and so on)

Directions

1. On a cookie sheet or pizza pan, press cookie dough into a thin circle about 12 inches wide. Bake at 375° F for 12 minutes or until golden brown. Cool. Place on serving tray.

2. Combine cream cheese, sugar, and vanilla. Mix until well blended. Spread over crust. Slice and arrange fruit over cream cheese mixture. Mix marmalade and water. Pour over fruit. Chill. Cut into wedges to serve.

Vocabulary Skills

Recipes often use short forms of words called **abbreviations**. Match the abbreviations in the box with their common recipe words.

C.	**tsp.**
oz.	**pkg.**

1. teaspoon _____

2. cup _____

3. ounce _____

4. package _____

Write these words so that they mean more than one.

5. ounce _____

6. teaspoon _____

7. minute _____

8. tray _____

9. sheet _____

10. circle _____

Reading Skills

Write these steps in the correct order. (Not all of the recipe's steps are here.)

• chill

• bake dough

• press dough into circle

• slice and arrange fruit

• make cream cheese mixture

1. _____

2. _____

3. _____

4. _____

5. _____

New Neighbors

Read to see what Yuki discovers.

1   The grass looked shiny. It had rained last night, but now the sun was shining brightly. If Yuki looked just right, she could even see little sparkles. She waded out into the grass to see if she could catch one.

2   Just as she bent down near a sparkle, she saw a girl looking at her over the fence. Yuki stopped. The girl waved her fingers a little bit. Yuki waved back a little bit and stood up.

3   Just then, Yuki's mom stepped out the back door. "Oh, hello. Yuki, this must be Roxie. I was just talking to her mom in the front yard." The girl nodded.

4   "Do you want to see my sunflowers?" asked Roxie. Yuki looked at her mom, then nodded. She went to the fence. In the corner of Roxie's yard, she saw the tallest flowers she had ever seen in her whole life.

Vocabulary Skills

Circle the word in each pair that has a long vowel sound like the sound in *mean* or *phone*.

1. seen   sent

2. bus   bone

3. worth   whole

4. getting   green

Add **'s** to show that something belongs to someone. Write the new words.

5. The grass belongs to Yuki.

   It is _____ grass.

6. The house belongs to Mom.

   It is _____ house.

Reading Skills

1. This story is mostly about

   _____ a girl playing in the wet grass.

   _____ how a rain storm hurt some plants.

   _____ two neighbor girls and how they meet.

Some words make us feel better than other words. For example, look at these sentences.

   I had some <u>mushy</u> ice cream.

   I had some <u>soft</u> ice cream.

If you're like most people, mushy ice cream doesn't sound very good to you. The word *mushy* makes us think of rotten things.

Read each sentence below. Think about the underlined words. Put a check mark next to the sentence that gives you better feelings.

2. _____ The grass looked <u>shiny</u>.

   _____ The grass looked <u>wet</u>.

3. _____ Yuki's mom <u>stepped</u> out.

   _____ Yuki's mom <u>stomped</u> out.

4. _____ The flowers were <u>skinny</u>.

   _____ The flowers were <u>narrow</u>.

The Sunflower House

Can you imagine a sunflower house?

Follow these directions to make your own sunflower house.

1. Choose a sunny space for a garden. Get permission from a grown-up to use the space.

2. Lay down a string to outline your garden. You may make a round or square space.

3. Dig a small ditch around the inside of your string. (You may need a grown-up to help.) Chop or rake the soil so it is fine and smooth.

4. In your ditch, place one sunflower seed about every nine inches. Go all the way around the circle. Then, remove one seed. That spot will be your doorway.

5. Brush soil over the seeds with your fingers. Press gently all around the ditch. Then, water and wait for your house to grow.

6 inches

5 feet

Vocabulary Skills

A word part that makes one sound is a **syllable**. The word *sun* has one syllable. The word *funny* has two syllables. Words, like *funny* or *halted*, that have two consonants between two vowels, are divided between the consonants: *fun / ny*, *hal / ted*. Draw a line to divide each word below into syllables.

1. g a r d e n

2. s u n n y

3. v i l l a g e

4. b e r r y

Circle the three words in each line that belong together.

5. round   large   square   oval

6. soil   dirt   mud   seed

7. sunflower   bird   rose   daisy

8. rake   hoe   shovel   bush

Reading Skills

1. What did you think of when you read the title, "The Sunflower House"?

_____

_____

2. Was your idea anything like the sunflower house described in the directions? Explain.

_____

_____

Study Skills

1. What information is given only in the diagram?

_____

_____

2. Would you have been able to follow the directions without the diagram? Explain.

_____

_____

Great Seats

What does David like best about his day with Grandfather?

1   People were rushing along the sidewalk. David stayed close to Grandfather. He kept his eyes on the signs that read, "To Stadium."

2   "I'm afraid we don't have very good seats, David," said Grandfather. "They're quite high up in the stands."

3   "That's okay, Grandfather," said David. He didn't really care about good seats. He was just glad to be here.

4   David and Grandfather ate popcorn and cheered for all of their favorite players. They saw some great hits and some great plays. During some innings, nothing happened. They cheered anyway.

5   After the game, David walked next to Grandfather. He could still see the players out on the green grass. He could smell the popcorn. He could hear the *smack* as the ball landed in the catcher's mitt.

6   "Grandfather," said David, smiling, "you were right. Those weren't *very good* seats—they were *great* seats."

NAME _____

Vocabulary Skills

The missing word in each sentence sounds like *match*. Change the **m** in *match* to **c**, **l**, or **p**. Fill in the blanks.

1. I watered the _____ of new grass.

2. Remember to close the _____.

3. He didn't make the _____.

Circle the best word for each sentence. Then, write it in the blank.

4. The game began with, "Let's _____ ball!"

 play   plow   plain

5. The batter _____ at the ball.

 sled   slowed   swung

6. The game was a _____ come true.

 dream   drew   dress

Reading Skills

1. Why is David's grandfather afraid?

 _____

 _____

2. How does David feel about the seats at first, and then later?

 _____

 _____

 _____

3. What three things does David remember?

 _____

 _____

 _____

4. What sights, smells, and sounds do you remember from a special day?

 _____

 _____

Baseball Basics

What do you know about the game of baseball?

1   To enjoy baseball, you need to know a few things.

2   There are nine sections, or *innings*, in a game. During an inning, each team gets a turn to bat and a turn to field.

3   When a team is at bat, one player at a time tries to hit the ball. When a player hits the ball, he runs around the bases, trying not to be tagged out by a fielder with the ball. The runner may stop at first, second, or third base and be "safe." If he makes it all the way to home base, he scores a run.

4   If a fielder catches the ball before it bounces, the batter is "out." If the ball touches the ground, a fielder must get the ball and tag the runner or throw the ball to another fielder who can do so. When three players have made outs, the teams trade places and the game goes on.

Vocabulary Skills

Write the words from the story that have these meanings.

1. sections of a baseball game

_____
(Par. 2)

2. a group of people

_____
(Par. 3)

3. springs back

_____
(Par. 4)

Circle the word that is the opposite of the underlined word.

4. <u>enjoy</u>   dislike   choose   hope

5. <u>lose</u>   hit   win   turn

6. <u>run</u>   tag   walk   trade

Reading Skills

1. What did you learn about baseball after you read this article?

_____

_____

_____

2. What happens during an inning?

_____

_____

3. What can a runner do to be safe?

_____

_____

4. Why do you think the author wrote this article?

_____ to give information

_____ to entertain

Baseball Cards

Read to learn about collecting baseball cards.

1 In 1887, the first baseball cards were printed. The earliest fans of baseball liked to collect the cards of their favorite players. In time, they collected cards of whole teams. Most of these early collectors were adults. In fact, they were businessmen who had the time and money to go to games during the week.

2 As baseball grew and changed, so did card collecting. As the game became more popular, it caught the interest of children, and so did collecting cards. A pack of cards and some candy cost just a few pennies in the early 1900s.

3 Today, some people pay thousands of dollars for very special or rare cards. For some, though, it is still a thrill to pay a few dollars for a pack of baseball cards, just to see what's inside.

NAME _____

Vocabulary Skills

Check the meaning that fits the underlined word in each sentence.

1. The <u>fans</u> took their seats.

_____ machines that blow air

_____ people who support a team

2. He had ten <u>sets</u> of cards.

_____ groups that fit together

_____ parts of a tennis match

Circle the best word for each sentence. Then, write it in the blank.

3. We waited eagerly for the first _____.

inch   pitch   branch

4. I would be afraid to _____ and miss!

swing   bring   fling

5. I slept through the _____ inning.

ninth   truth   cloth

Reading Skills

Put each word in the right blank.

adults	collect	rare

1. How much is a _____ card worth?

2. Only _____ could pay that much!

3. Many people like to _____ cards.

4. This article is mostly about

_____ the greatest baseball teams.

_____ the history of baseball.

_____ collecting baseball cards.

5. Do you collect anything? Write about it.

_____

_____

Spectrum Reading Grade 2

91

Those Were the Days

What does Lorna learn about the past?

1   "Who's that in the picture?" Lorna asked. She pointed to a woman with white hair. Her mother looked more closely.

2   "That's your great-grandmother Lucy."

3   Lorna looked closer too. "How did she ride her air scooter in that thing she's wearing?"

4   Lorna's mother smiled. "That 'thing' is a dress. And they didn't have air scooters. People drove cars to get around."

5   "Oh, I remember reading about those," Lorna nodded. "How did people get them up to their houses?"

6   "Lorna's mother smiled again. "People's houses were on the ground back then."

7   Lorna made a face. "That would be weird."

Vocabulary Skills

Circle the best word for each sentence. Then, write it in the blank.

1. Great-grandmother Lucy had white _____.

   pair   flair   hair

2. She wore a _____.

   class   dress   miss

3. Lorna didn't understand about the _____.

   blouse   house   mouse

Each of these words has an ending. Underline the base words.

4. pointed

5. closely

6. wearing

7. houses

Reading Skills

Some of these sentences are about **real** things. Write **R** by them. The other sentences are about **make-believe** things. Write **M** by them.

1. _____ Houses are not on the ground.

2. _____ Children wear space suits.

3. _____ People look at old pictures.

4. What do you learn about Lorna from the picture?

   _____

   _____

5. Why does Lorna ask about getting a car up to a house?

   _____

   _____

6. Look at the picture. What do you like best about Lorna's world?

   _____

One City Block

Read to see who lives on Rachel's block.

1   Mama says the whole world lives right here on our block. Everyone is different, and I'll always like it that way.

2   Right down the hall is Mrs. Rotollo. She and her husband speak Italian, but when they see me, they always say "hello" in English. When Mama was sick once, Mrs. Rotollo helped me make dinner. It turned out yummy!

3   Upstairs is Philip. He takes dancing lessons. When I hear his feet thumping in the morning, I know it is time to get up.

4   Next door is Mr. Tran's grocery. Mama sends me over for fresh vegetables and fruit. Mr. Tran always picks out the best ones for me.

5   On the first floor of our building is Mrs. Moya's shop. I love the colors! I always know when it's going to rain because she takes her piñatas down.

Vocabulary Skills

Write the story words that have the same meanings as these words.

1. entire

   _____
   (Par. 1)

2. good-tasting

   _____
   (Par. 2)

3. unwell

   _____
   (Par. 2)

4. new

   _____
   (Par. 4)

Write a word from the story that stands for each pair of words.

5. I will _____

6. it is _____

Reading Skills

Write one thing you know about each of Rachel's neighbors.

1. Mr. and Mrs. Rotollo

   _____

   _____

2. Philip

   _____

   _____

3. Mr. Tran

   _____

   _____

4. Mrs. Moya

   _____

   _____

5. Look at the picture and the story. Which neighbor seems most interesting to you? Write why.

   _____

   _____

What Is a City?

What kinds of people, buildings, and jobs make up your city?

1   A city is made up of people. They live and work in the city. Some of them work to make sure the city is a good place to live. They make rules for the people in the city. One rule might be, "Don't throw trash in the street." What rules does your city have?

2   Other people try to make sure there are things to do in a city. They run restaurants, movie theaters, and sports centers. The bigger a city is, the more things there are to do. What is there to do in your city?

3   If a city is going to be a nice place to live, the people who live there must agree to follow the city's rules. They must also pay taxes. Taxes pay for things such as cleaning the streets, running schools, and filling the public library with books. Is your city a nice place to live?

Vocabulary Skills

Write the words from the article that have these meanings.

I. garbage

_____
(Par. 1)

2. places to eat

_____
(Par. 2)

3. go along with

_____
(Par. 3)

The missing words in these sentences contain the letters **oa**. Fill in the blanks.

4. The mayor rode a _____ in the parade.

5. The street is lined with _____ trees.

6. Even the plow could not get up our icy _____.

7. We take our _____ to the lake.

Reading Skills

I. This article is mostly about

_____ what makes a city.

_____ how to live in a city.

_____ America's largest cities.

2. What is your favorite thing to do in your city or in a nearby city? Write about it.

_____

_____

_____

3. The person who wrote this article is the _____.

4. Do you think this article is meant to give information or to make you laugh? Write why.

_____

_____

_____

_____

Ant and Grasshopper

What does Grasshopper learn?

1   Ant hurried back and forth. Each time he went, he carried another small piece of food back to his nest. *I have to fill the nest, I have to fill the nest*, he panted to himself as he worked.

2   Grasshopper watched. He thought Ant was silly. "Come watch the bugs skate on the pond," he called to Ant.

3   Ant didn't even stop. "Oh, no, I can't. I must get more food for winter. I have to fill the nest."

4   So it went all summer. Grasshopper called out every day, and Ant answered the same.

5   When the leaves had all fallen off the trees, a sharp wind began to blow. Ant crawled safely into his nest. Grasshopper had nowhere to go.

6   In spring, when fresh green buds came on the trees, Ant came out of his nest. Grasshopper was nowhere to be found.

Vocabulary Skills

Read each sentence and circle the word that is made of two shorter words. Write the two words on the lines.

1. In the story, who had nowhere to go in winter?

_____ _____

2. Ant talked to himself as he worked.

_____ _____

3. Grasshopper did not get ready for winter.

_____ _____

The word ending **-est** means *most*, as in *luckiest*. Add **est** to each underlined word to change its meaning.

4. Ant was <u>smart</u>. _____

5. Mole was <u>soft</u>. _____

6. Grasshopper could jump <u>high</u>. _____

Reading Skills

Some of these sentences are about **real** things. Write **R** by them. The other sentences are about **make-believe** things. Write **M** by them.

1. _____ Ants gather food.

2. _____ Grasshoppers watch baseball games.

3. _____ Grasshoppers are lazy.

4. This story is called a **fable**. Fables usually teach a lesson. What lesson does this one teach?

_____

_____

_____

5. If you were Ant, what would you have said to Grasshopper?

_____

_____

_____

A Pleasant Tale

Read to see what the princess learns from the market girl.

1   The king had made a law. The people in the town had to be pleasant to the princess. Each day, the princess stood on the castle wall so everyone could be pleasant to her. Each day, a few people looked up pleasantly. No one waved or smiled. This made the princess sad and mad.

2   One day, she noticed a market girl in the marketplace. The market girl waved and everyone she met waved back to her. They smiled. They looked pleasant. The princess had the girl brought to the castle.

3   "Why do people wave and smile at you? Why are they pleasant?" demanded the princess.

4   The market girl thought this was a silly question. "Perhaps it is because I wave and smile at them," she said pleasantly.

5   The next day, the princess stood on the castle wall and waved. She even smiled. Down in the marketplace, the market girl waved and smiled back. This made the princess happy.

Vocabulary Skills

Circle the word that has a short vowel sound like the one in the underlined word.

1. <u>king</u>   smiled   silly

2. <u>castle</u>   waved   happy

3. <u>met</u>   dress   few

4. <u>sad</u>   day   mad

Reading Skills

1. How did the princess feel when she waved and no one waved back?

_____

2. How did the princess speak to the market girl?

_____ She spoke pleasantly.

_____ She spoke angrily.

_____ She begged her.

3. What lesson did the princess learn from the market girl?

_____

_____

Study Skills

Number the words to show A-B-C order for each list.

4. _____ pleasant

_____ wave

_____ market

_____ sad

5. _____ smile

_____ princess

_____ castle

_____ happy

Castles

What do you already know about castles?

Why do castles have walls?

1   Have you ever seen a castle without walls? They all seem to have them, don't they? The walls are for protection. At least, they used to be. Hundreds of years ago, the main reason for building a castle was to protect yourself from your enemies.

Why do castle walls have notches?

2   What if your enemies attacked you? You couldn't just hide. You probably had to fight back. So you sent your knights or the townspeople up to the walls. They may have had rocks to throw or arrows to shoot. Either way, they took aim through the openings, or the lower parts of the notches. They stood behind the higher parts of the notches to protect themselves from whatever the enemy was throwing or shooting back up at them.

Vocabulary Skills

Look at these words. They are broken into syllables. Sound out each syllable. Then, say the words aloud.

1. protection pro / tec / tion

2. enemies e / ne / mies

The word ending **-er** means *more*. So, *higher* means *more high*. Add **er** to each underlined word to change its meaning.

3. Our castle wall is <u>thick</u>.

_____

4. Their castle wall is <u>tall</u>.

_____

5. His castle wall is <u>strong</u>.

_____

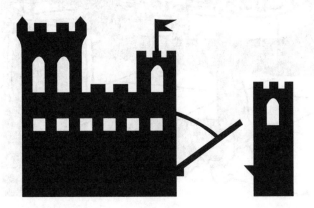

Reading Skills

1. How are castles different from our homes? List some ways.

Castles

Walls _____

_____

Purpose _____

_____

Our Homes

Walls _____

_____

Purpose _____

_____

2. Imagine that you are standing on the wall of the castle shown on page 102. Describe what you see.

_____

_____

_____

_____

Yard Sale Day

How does this yard sale turn out?

1   The day we had our yard sale is a day I'll never forget. Early on that Saturday morning, we set everything out neatly on tables. People started coming. Some of them bought things, some didn't.

2   All at once, the sky got very dark. Mom took one look and told Nathan and me to get into the garage. A big *whoosh* of wind came. Over went the bikes. Over went the tables. *Crash* went an old lamp. Within a few minutes, it was all over. We walked out of the garage, amazed by the huge mess.

3   I heard a door slam and looked up. Mr. Piper from down the street said it looked like we needed some help. Soon, a bunch of neighbors came to help. I don't remember how much we sold, but we ended up having the nicest neighborhood get-together ever! Maybe we should have a yard sale again next summer.

Vocabulary Skills

The missing word in each sentence sounds like *sale*. Change the **s** in *sale* to **g**, **p**, or **t**. Fill in the blanks.

1. The story made quite a _____ to tell.

2. The strong wind might have been a _____.

3. If you are afraid, you might be _____.

Reading Skills

1. What two things made this yard sale day a time to remember?

_____

_____

2. In the story, there is a problem. What is the problem and how is it solved?

Problem _____

_____

How it is solved _____

_____

3. Write **1**, **2**, **3**, and **4** by these sentences to show the correct order from the story.

_____ People began coming to the sale.

_____ Neighbors came to help.

_____ The storm blew through.

_____ The family set things out on tables.

4. The person who tells a story is the **narrator**. What did the narrator like best about the yard sale day?

_____

_____

_____

_____

_____

_____

Hard at Work

Why are these students working so hard?

1 Mrs. Davis looked around the room at her students. "I think it would be lovely for each of you to have flowers on your desk for the Open House."

2 A hand went up. "Yes, Caitlyn?" said Mrs. Davis.

3 "Can we give our flowers to our parents when they come?"

4 Mrs. Davis smiled. "Yes, I think that's a fine idea, Caitlyn."

5 Greg raised his hand. "Are there any more green pipe cleaners? I need some more flower stems."

6 "Yes, right here," said Mrs. Davis, and she handed more stems to Greg. "Does anyone need more coffee filters?"

7 No one answered. They were all working so hard that no one even heard the bell ring. School was over, but the students were all still hard at work.

Vocabulary Skills

Circle the best word for each sentence. Then, write the word in the blank.

1. The students were busy making _____.

   flowers   flakes   flutes

2. Greg asked for more _____ cleaners.

   point   part   pipe

3. No one even heard the _____ ring.

   bark   bowl   bell

Add 's to show that something belongs to someone. Write the new words.

4. The desk belongs to Mrs. Davis.

   It is Mrs. _____ desk.

5. The flower belongs to Greg.

   It is _____ flower.

6. The idea belongs to Caitlyn.

   It is _____ idea.

Reading Skills

1. Circle the word that best tells about Caitlyn.

   selfish   thoughtful   careless

2. Circle the word that best tells about Mrs. Davis.

   nice   nervous   angry

3. What parts of the story helped you learn about Mrs. Davis?

   _____

   _____

Study Skills

Number the words to show A-B-C order for each list.

1. _____ desk
   _____ students
   _____ room
   _____ flowers

2. _____ idea
   _____ parents
   _____ hand
   _____ working

Open House

What is there to see at the Open House?

1   "I want to show you my butterfly, and my flower poster, and...."

2   "Hey, slow down, Ted. We'll look at everything. Don't worry," said Ted's dad. Ted grinned. He was excited about showing everything in his classroom to his parents.

3   Ted led them around the room to his butterfly model, his flower poster, his plant report, and his part of the butterfly life cycle. At each stop, his parents said, "What a great job, Ted!" or "That's wonderful, Ted!"

4   At last, they stopped near Ted's desk. "These are for you," said Ted. He handed a handful of coffee-filter flowers to his mom. "Great job!" and "That's wonderful!" didn't seem to be enough, so Mom just gave Ted a hug.

Vocabulary Skills

To show more than one, add **s**. If a word ends in **y**, change the **y** to **i** and add **es**. So, *one fly* becomes *two flies*. Change the endings of these words to show that there are more than one.

1. one butterfly

   two_____

2. one lady

   two_____

3. one city

   two_____

Circle the best word for each sentence. Then, write it in the blank.

4. Unlike real flowers, fake flowers don't _____.

   draw   droop   drain

5. Jenny used _____ colors on her flower.

   crazy   crow   cream

6. Mom thought Ted's work was _____.

   grass   great   grin

Reading Skills

Put each word in the right blank.

excited	model	poster

1. The butterfly _____ even had wings that flapped.

2. Even Mrs. Davis was _____ about the Open House.

3. The picture on the _____ showed a sunflower.

4. This story is mostly about

   _____ how hard Mrs. Davis worked.

   _____ Ted and his parents at the Open House.

   _____ the parts of a butterfly.

5. Have you ever been excited about an Open House or a school project? Write about it.

   _____

   _____

   _____

   _____

Making Flowers

Learn how to make flowers out of coffee filters.

Supplies Needed

- white coffee filters
- watercolor paints
- cup of water
- paintbrushes
- spoon
- newspapers
- pipe cleaners

Instructions

1. Gather all supplies. Cover your work area with newspapers.

2. Flatten a coffee filter. Drip clean water onto the filter with a spoon.

3. Brush or drip watercolor paints onto the coffee filter. For bright colors, use more paint. For pale colors, use more water.

4. Let coffee filter dry.

5. Gather center of coffee filter and twist pipe cleaner around it several times.

Vocabulary Skills

Circle the three words in each row that belong together.

1. water   milk   cheese   juice

2. twist   drip   bend   curl

3. paper   center   edge   corner

Reading Skills

Write these steps in the correct order. (Not all of the steps are listed here.)

- flatten coffee filter

- drip paint onto coffee filter

- let dry

- gather supplies

- wet down coffee filter

1. _____

2. _____

3. _____

4. _____

5. _____

Study Skills

1. Which *Reading Skills* step does the illustration show?

_____

2. How did the illustration help you understand the project?

_____

_____

_____

_____

_____

_____

_____

_____

_____

_____

_____

Parts of a Plant

*Can you name the parts of
a plant?*

Root

The roots collect water and
food, or *nutrients,* from the soil.
The plant cannot grow without
roots or without the water
and nutrients.

Stem

The stem carries nutrients from
the roots to the leaves.

Leaf

The leaves collect energy from
the sun. Using this energy, plus
the water and nutrients from
the roots, the plant makes its
own food.

Seed

In the center of the flower,
seeds form. Birds eat some of
them. Others drop to the
ground and sprout new plants
next year.

Flower

Flowers produce seeds. Flowers'
bright petals appeal to birds
and butterflies. They spread
pollen, which is needed to form
the seeds.

Vocabulary Skills

The missing words in these sentences contain the letters **ee** or **ea**. Fill in the blanks.

1. Most plants begin from _____.

2. The biggest type of plant is a _____.

3. I don't want to rake even one more _____.

Reading Skills

1. What jobs do a plant's leaves do?

   _____

   _____

2. Write what nutrients are.

   _____

   _____

3. After the roots collect water and nutrients, what happens?

   _____

   _____

Study Skills

1. The illustration on page 112 includes **call-outs**, short pieces of information that explain parts of an illustration. How can you tell what each callout is telling about?

   _____

   _____

No Help for Allison

Why can't Mom help Allison?

1   Allison was bored. She had asked Mom to play a game with her, but Mom said she was busy.

2   Allison read for a while. Then, she was bored again. *Ugh, there's nothing to do!* she thought. She asked for help with her weaving, but Mom was busy. *Why is Mom always busy when I need her?* Now, Allison was bored and grumpy.

3   Allison shuffled into the kitchen. Mom looked up from her cooking. "Oh, Ally, I'm glad you're here. Come next door and help me cheer up Mrs. Baxter. She broke her leg last week, and I'm taking some food over to her."

4   "That's why you were busy?" asked Allison.

5   "That's right. Why?"

6   "Oh, poor Mrs. Baxter," said Allison, suddenly feeling not so grumpy. "I wanted you to help me today, but it turns out you were helping someone who really needed it."

Vocabulary Skills

Write the words from the article that have these meanings.

1. feeling tired and unhappy

_____
(Par. 1)

2. crabby

_____
(Par. 2)

3. dragged her feet

_____
(Par. 3)

Circle the word in each pair that has a long vowel sound like the sound of **a-e** in *make* or **ee** in *seem*.

5.	help	need
6.	weaving	else
7.	game	said
8.	day	had

Reading Skills

1. At the beginning of the story, how did you think it would turn out?

_____

_____

2. Why can't Mom help Allison?

_____

_____

3. How does Allison feel when she finds out what her mother was doing?

_____

_____

Why do you think she feels that way?

_____

_____

Write **T** if the sentence is true. Write **N** if the story does not give the information.

4. _____ Mom is kind to a neighbor.

_____ Mom dislikes playing games with Allison.

_____ Mom is a great cook.

_____ Mom uses a nickname for her daughter.

Can Central

What is Mark and Timo's problem?

1   Mark was used to people staring. He stopped his bike, picked up the soda can on the sidewalk, and tossed it into the special basket on his bike. He flashed a smile at the people staring, just to confuse them.

2   At home, Timo was waiting outside the garage. He also had a basket full of cans on his bike. The boys nodded at each other, then opened the garage door. A mountain of black, can-filled garbage bags greeted them. Mark and Timo had been here every day, emptying their baskets into the bags. Now, the summer was almost over. It was time to figure out how to get all of their cans to the recycling center.

Vocabulary Skills

A word part that makes one sound is a **syllable**. The word *but* has one syllable. The word *butter* has two syllables. Words, like *butter*, that have two consonants between two vowels, are divided between the consonants: *but / ter*. Draw a line to divide each word below into syllables.

1. b a s k e t

2. c o r n e r

3. c o n f u s e

4. n o d d e d

5. s u m m e r

Circle the word that is the opposite of the underlined word.

6. <u>outside</u>   special   inside   every

7. <u>opened</u>   closed   filled   tossed

Reading Skills

Some words create pictures in our minds. For example, look at these sentences.

Mark <u>rode</u> his bike around the block.

Mark <u>zoomed</u> his bike around the block.

Rode tells you what Mark did, but *zoomed* really tells you how he did it and how he looked as he did it.

Read each sentence below. Think about the underlined words. Make a check mark next to the sentence that really tells you what the character did or how something looks.

1. _____ Mark <u>put</u> a can into his basket.

   _____ Mark <u>tossed</u> a can into his basket.

2. _____ He <u>flashed</u> a smile.

   _____ He <u>smiled</u>.

Trading Favors

Read to see what Mark and Timo figure out.

1 It's funny how things work out sometimes. Mark and Timo had been stuck. They had all these cans and no way to get them to the recycling center. They went for a walk and ran into a neighbor, Mr. Timmons. He was stuck, too. He explained how he had hurt his foot and had to use a cane. He was trying to figure out how to get his lawn mowed.

2 The boys offered to help. Mr. Timmons was very grateful. Then, it happened. He opened his garage and asked the boys if they could dump the grass clippings into the back of his truck. A truck!

3 "Mr. Timmons," said Mark, "how would you feel about doing us a favor?" After Mark and Timo explained, Mr. Timmons said he would be more than happy to trade favors.

Vocabulary Skills

Write the story words that have the same meanings as these words.

1. told

_____
(Par. 1)

2. thankful

_____
(Par. 2)

3. put or throw

_____
(Par. 2)

4. act of kindness

_____
(Par. 3)

Circle the best word for each sentence. Then, write it in the blank.

5. Timo could not _____ of a way.

thick   think   thank

6. The boys _____ the clippings into the truck.

thing   third   threw

7. They ran into Mr. Timmons by _____.

change   chance   chain

Reading Skills

1. Why did the boys take a walk?

_____

_____

2. Why did Mr. Timmons need help with his lawn?

_____

_____

Look at the picture. Put a check mark by the two sentences that tell about the picture.

3. _____ Mr. Timmons is asleep.

_____ Mr. Timmons uses a cane.

_____ Mr. Timmons is wearing jeans.

Counting Money

What will the boys do with the money they earned?

1 It was a hot, muggy day. Mark and Timo were glad they weren't lugging cans today. Yesterday, it had taken hours to get all of the cans they had collected to the recycling center. Mr. Timmons said his truck hadn't worked so hard in a long time. He was laughing when he said it, though.

2 Today, all the boys had to do was count their money and figure out what to do with it. They talked about bikes and basketballs. They dreamed about rockets and hot air balloons.

3 As they walked, Mark bent over and picked up a can without even thinking about it. When he saw the can in his hand, he laughed.

4 "Old habits die hard," Timo said. "Maybe we better buy some more trash bags!"

Vocabulary Skills

The prefix **re-** means *again*. Add **re** to the beginning of these words to complete these sentences.

1. The boys had to _____count their money.

2. Maybe they should _____cycle more cans.

Circle the letters that complete each word. Then, write the letters in the blank.

3. Mark and Timo worked h_____d on the lawn.

   ar   er   ur

4. Timo could only imagine being in a hot a_____ balloon.

   or   ir   ar

5. They will certainly need m_____e trash bags.

   ar   or   er

Reading Skills

1. What did the boys do yesterday?

   _____

2. Today, the boys are

   _____.

3. How did Mr. Timmons feel about helping the boys?

   _____

   _____

4. What part of the story helped you answer question **3**?

   _____

   _____

5. After Mark picked up the can, he laughed because

   _____

   _____.

6. What does "old habits die hard" mean? Do you think it is true?

   _____

   _____

Spending Money

Read to see what choice Mark and Timo make.

1   Mark and Timo were still laughing about picking up cans when they caught up with Mr. Timmons.

2   "Hi, Mr. Timmons," smiled Timo. "Where are you headed?"

3   Mr. Timmons seemed pleased to see them. "Well, it's Thursday, so I'm on my way to help at the food pantry."

4   "What goes on there?" Mark asked.

5   "Oh, they always need help packing or unpacking cans of food," Mr. Timmons explained. "The pantry helps those people who don't have the money to buy food for their families."

6   "Not enough money for food?" said the boys together. They looked at each other and nodded.

7   "Can we come along, Mr. Timmons?" asked Timo. "I think we just figured out what to do with our recycling money."

Vocabulary Skills

Circle the best word for each sentence. Then, write it in the blank.

1. Mr. Timmons seemed
   _____.

   pleased   ended   bread

2. He still needs his _____.

   tune   shine   cane

3. Mr. Timmons is glad to
   _____.

   trap   help   drop

To show more than one, add **s** to the word. Some words don't follow that pattern, though. Use the words in the box to complete each sentence. Then, write the singular form of the word on the line after each sentence.

| **people**   **children** |
| **mice** |

4. Mark saw two _____ in the garage. _____

5. Mr. Timmons likes _____.
   _____

6. Many _____ help at the food pantry. _____

Reading Skills

1. This story is mostly about

   _____ how a food pantry
   works.

   _____ what Mr. Timmons
   does in his free time.

   _____ what the boys decide
   to do with their money.

2. Mr. Timmons is going to

   _____.

3. What will Mr. Timmons
   do there?

   _____

4. Mr. Timmons says something
   that gives the boys an idea.
   What does he say?

   _____

   _____

You Can Recycle

Why is recycling a good idea?

1 Here's a riddle. What can you use over and over again? An aluminum can.

2 In fact, about half of the aluminum cans you see in the grocery store are recycled. As little as 60 days ago, that aluminum can in the store could have been part of some other can in some other store. If you buy that can, empty it, and recycle it, it could be part of another aluminum can 60 days from now.

3 Recycling aluminum cans saves energy. Making a can out of recycled aluminum uses only a small part of the energy it takes to make a can out of new aluminum.

4 Recycling saves energy and money, and it cuts down on waste. Recycling aluminum makes sense no matter how you look at it.

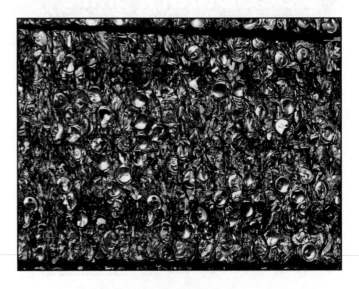

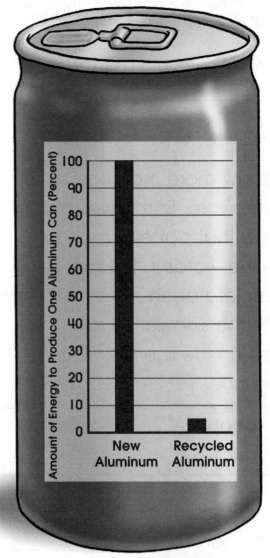

Vocabulary Skills

Circle the word that means the opposite of the underlined word.

1. <u>empty</u>   again   use   full

2. <u>save</u>   part   waste   buy

Write the words from the article that have these meanings.

3. one of two equal parts

_____
(Par. 2)

4. pay money for

_____
(Par. 2)

5. power

_____
(Par. 3)

6. what is thrown away

_____
(Par. 4)

Reading Skills

1. This article is mostly about

_____ cans at the grocery store.

_____ recycling aluminum cans.

_____ how to recycle aluminum.

2. If you buy a can of lemonade, drink it, and recycle it, how long will it take for that can to be recycled and made into new cans?

_____

3. It makes sense to recycle because _____

_____.

Study Skills

1. What does the graph show?

_____

_____

2. Why do you think the author included a graph with this article?

_____

_____

Pool Rules

What do the girls learn?

1   At eleven o'clock this morning, the city pool opened for the season. At two minutes after eleven, Katie and Sara were in the girls' locker room. They wanted to be the first ones into the pool.

2   "I'll race you!" yelled Sara as she dashed out the locker room door. Katie was right behind her. They were halfway across the hot cement when they heard *phweeeet!* "Walk, please!"

3   Katie slowed and turned toward the lifeguard. She felt terrible. She knew they shouldn't have been running. At that moment, her foot went out from under her. Down she went, backward and sideway all at the same time. Ouch! Her elbow scraped on the cement.

4   Sara and the lifeguard were beside her in an instant. "Are you okay, Katie?"

5   Katie made a face. "I think so, but next time I think I'll walk."

Vocabulary Skills

Each of these words has an ending. Underline the base words.

1. wanted

2. yelled

3. dashed

4. turned

For most words that end in **e**, drop the **e** before adding **ed** or **ing**. Add the endings **-ed** and **-ing** to these words. Remember to drop the **e** first. One is done for you.

scrape + ed ____**scraped**____

scrape + ing ____**scraping**____

5. race + ed _____

race + ing _____

6. trade + ed _____

trade + ing _____

Write a word from the story that stands for each pair of words.

7. I will _____

8. should not _____

Reading Skills

Choose the best word to finish each sentence below. Write the word in the blank.

1. The girls want to be the _____ ones into the pool.

dash   first   next

2. Katie slowed down when the whistle _____.

blew   cool   walk

3. Katie hurt her elbow when she _____.

feet   backward   fell

4. What rule do you think Katie and Sara were breaking?

_____

5. Why do you think most pools have this rule?

_____

_____

6. What else do you know about pool rules?

_____

_____

Hot Wool

Why isn't it a good idea to wear a wool sweater on a hot day?

1   I peered into my drawer. *What should I wear today? Ah! That's it!* I dove down to find my favorite red sweater way at the bottom. That sweater always made me feel good. I pulled it on and headed for the kitchen.

2   "Hi, Mom. May I go over to Nick's house?" I asked.

3   "Sure, Ryan," she said, but then she looked up. "Hey, do you really think you need a wool sweater today?"

4   I looked down. I loved this sweater. Why did it matter that it was wool?

5   "Wool clothing is made for warmth," Mom went on. "It's 90 degrees out there. You'll roast." I promised to come back and change if I got hot. Mom raised an eyebrow, but she said okay.

6   I was back in about five minutes. Mom was right.

Vocabulary Skills

Write the words from the story that have these meanings.

1. looked carefully

_____
(Par. 1)

2. most liked

_____
(Par. 1)

3. hair from sheep

_____
(Par. 3)

4. an amount of heat

_____
(Par. 5)

In each sentence, circle each word that has the same vowel sound as the underlined word.

5. headed
Ryan's favorite sweater was red.

6. Nick
This is Ryan's friend.

7. Mom
She thinks Ryan will get hot.

8. back
Ryan was glad to change shirts.

Reading Skills

1. What did you think as Ryan was finding his favorite sweater? Did it seem like a good idea?

_____

_____

2. Are there any clues in the picture that tell you it is a hot day? What are they?

_____

_____

_____

3. What causes Mom to raise her eyebrow?

_____

_____

_____

4. Why does Ryan come back home?

_____

_____

From Sheep to Sweater

What do you know about wool?

1   Have you ever wondered how the wool gets from the sheep to your sweater? Let's find out.

2   First, the sheep gets a haircut. This is called **shearing** the sheep. The wool from each sheep comes off in nearly one big piece, called a **fleece**.

3   The fleece is then washed. Washing removes straw and dirt. Washing also gets rid of a special oil that helps keep the sheep dry. When it is dry, the clean fleece is combed, or **carded**. Carding makes the wool soft and fluffy.

4   Next, the carded wool is made into yarn. This is done by **spinning**, which twists the wool into a long, thin strand. Finally, someone can use the yarn to knit your sweater.

Vocabulary Skills

You will find the words below in **bold** print in the article. Find the words and read carefully. Then, write the meaning of each word.

I. shearing _____

2. fleece _____

3. carded _____

4. spinning _____

Add **'s** to show that a thing belongs to someone or something. Write the new words.

5. The wool belongs to the sheep.

It is the _____ wool.

6. The oil belongs to the fleece.

It is the _____ oil.

7. The yarn belongs to the spinner.

It is the _____ yarn.

Reading Skills

Write these steps in the correct order.

- Dry the fleece.

- Shear the sheep.

- Card the fleece.

- Spin wool into yarn.

- Wash the fleece.

I. _____

2. _____

3. _____

4. _____

5. _____

6. The author wrote this article to

_____ give information.

_____ make you laugh.

7. Choose the photo you like best. Tell what is happening in the photo.

_____

Cotton: From Field to Closet

Read to see how your cotton clothing is made.

1   Are you wearing jeans or a t-shirt today? Chances are good that some part of your clothing is made out of cotton. How do those puffy little cotton balls out in the field get to your closet?

2   First, those white cotton balls are, in fact, fine hairs growing out of many tiny seeds. After the cotton is picked, it is cleaned and dried. Then, the cotton is separated from the seeds. A machine called a *cotton gin* does this. The ginned cotton is then pressed into 500-pound bales and sent to a mill.

3   At the mill, the cotton is spun into yarn or thread. Then, huge mechanical looms weave the thread into fabric. Finally, the cloth is cut and sewed to make a shirt or a pair of jeans, just like yours.

Vocabulary Skills

In each row, circle the letters in each word that make the same sound you hear in the underlined word.

jeans f(ee)l sw(ee)t n(ea)t

1. those   coast   owner   goal

2. seeds   field   wheel   eager

3. pound   crown   ounce   pout

Look at these words. They are broken into syllables. Sound out each syllable. Then, say the word aloud.

4. mechanical
me / chan / i / cal

5. fabric
fab / ric

6. separated
sep / a / rat / ed

Reading Skills

Words such as *it, you,* and *they* take the place of other words. Read these sentences. Then, fill in the blanks.

1. After the cotton is picked, it is cleaned and dried.

   It stands for _____.

2. Cotton pickers used to wear gloves when they worked.

   They stands for _____.

3. Imagine that you are holding a cotton ball. It has many little seeds in it. Does it seem as if it would be easy to get those seeds out? Explain.

   _____

   _____

4. Before the cotton gin was invented, people had to remove cotton seeds by hand. Would you want that job? Write why or why not.

   _____

Baxter's Shoes

Where would you look for missing shoes?

1 "I was sure I put them in my closet," I said to Mom.

2 "Well, maybe you should look again," Mom smiled, but she didn't get up to help. I knew the rule. If the shoes go on your feet, you keep track of them. I guess she was right. She never asked me where her shoes were. I kept looking.

3 The front hall, the back porch, and the basement were next. Then, I looked under my bed, in the corner of the kitchen, and by the family room sofa.

4 A thump from the corner made me look over at Baxter. He was on his bed thumping his tail. And there under his paw were my shoes!

5 "Baxter! Those are *my* shoes. Why are *you* keeping track of them?"

Vocabulary Skills

Put a check mark by the meaning that fits the underlined word in each sentence.

1. <u>Well</u>, I thought I looked there.

_____ a hole for water

_____ a word that people say when they begin speaking

2. The shoes were only a few <u>feet</u> from me.

_____ a unit of measure

_____ body parts

3. He had to <u>track</u> his shoes to find them.

_____ to follow a trail

_____ a path

4. He went <u>back</u> into the kitchen.

_____ to go again

_____ rear part of human body

The missing word in each sentence sounds like *paw*. Change the **p** in *paw* to **cl**, **gn**, or **r**. Fill in the blanks.

5. I hope Baxter didn't _____ on the shoes.

6. I think I see a _____ mark.

7. Does Baxter like shoes cooked or _____?

Reading Skills

1. Most stories include a problem. What is this story's problem?

_____

2. As you began to read "Baxter's Shoes," who did you think Baxter was?

_____

3. The **narrator** is the person who tells a story. Whom does the narrator ask for help?

_____

Getting Ready

How does Andrea get ready for the game?

1   Andrea's teacher, Mrs. McKay, was all excited about it. The yearly kickball game against Mr. Haskins' class was tomorrow. Andrea had an icky feeling in her stomach. She didn't know how to play kickball, and she wasn't sure she wanted to learn.

2   After Andrea came home from school, her mom could tell something was wrong. Andrea told her about the game.

3   "We can fix that," said Mom, opening the back door. "Welcome to the backyard kickball field." An hour later, Andrea had practiced pitching, kicking, fielding, and running the bases. She had won the game, even without any teammates. Mom had been a really good sport about it. Now, Andrea was ready for tomorrow!

NAME _____

Vocabulary Skills

Read each sentence and circle the word that is made of two shorter words. Write the two words on the lines.

1. A backyard practice was just what Andrea needed.

_____ _____

2. Andrea was more than ready for kickball now.

_____ _____

3. She learned something from her mother.

_____ _____

4. Playing with mom is okay, but playing with teammates is even better.

_____ _____

Reading Skills

Find words in the story with these meanings.

1. once every twelve months

_____
(Par. 1)

2. find out, get information

_____
(Par. 1)

3. area of open ground

_____
(Par. 3)

4. Andrea is worried because

_____

_____.

5. Put a check mark by the sentence that best tells about how Andrea looks in the picture.

_____ Andrea is lazy.

_____ Andrea thinks kickball is funny.

_____ Andrea is working hard.

6. What lesson did Andrea learn?

Things work out if

_____ you keep things to yourself.

_____ you let people help you.

_____ you never let anyone see you have a problem.

Spectrum Reading Grade 2

137

Fitness for Life

How do you keep yourself healthy?

Healthful Lifestyle

¹ Experts agree a well-rounded healthful lifestyle is the best way to be healthy. You can't just watch what you eat. You can't just exercise. You have to eat well and exercise.

Eat well

² Choose wisely from among the four food groups. These groups are fruit and vegetables, bread, dairy, and meat. Do not snack on sweet or salty foods between meals. Also, drink eight glasses of water a day.

Exercise

³ Exercising regularly at least three times each week is the best plan. If that's just not possible, at least be active. Use stairs instead of elevators. Walk the last few blocks to school or work. Take a walk instead of watching television. Make healthy choices.

Vocabulary Skills

Circle the best word for each sentence. Then, write it in the blank.

1. Good exercise will help you
_____.

grow   gray   group

2. Eating many different kinds of foods is _____.

smoky   smart   smell

3. Slow down, don't eat so
_____.

quickly   quiet   quilt

The sentences below all have underlined pairs of words that begin with the same letter. One word in each pair is missing. Fill in the blanks.

4. It is important to <u>eat</u> well and _____ to stay healthy.

5. Choose from among the <u>four</u> _____ groups.

6. Do not snack on <u>sweet</u> or _____ foods between meals.

Reading Skills

1. This article is mostly about what?

_____ It is important to eat the right foods.

_____ Make sure you exercise every day.

_____ Eat well and exercise to stay healthy.

2. If people don't have time to exercise, what can they do to stay active? Write two ideas.

_____

_____

3. What do you do to stay healthy?

_____

_____

_____

Snow Rooms

Read about a great snow day.

1   It was a magical day. I woke up and looked out the window. Everything was white. It had snowed a ton during the night. I didn't even have to ask about school. There was no way!

2   By 8 o'clock, my sister and I were out in it. We went to the top of a little hill and jumped down. We knew there was a hollow under all that drifted snow. By pushing against the snow with our shoulders, we were able to widen our holes into spaces. Before long, the spaces became two rooms with a door between them.

3   We fixed up our rooms with snow benches, and I even made a snow picture on the wall. We lost all track of time. Mom finally came and got us. But first, she had some snow lunch with us in our snow rooms.

Vocabulary Skills

The missing word in each sentence contains the letters **ow**. Fill in the blanks.

1. I looked out the _____ right away.

2. Everything was covered with _____.

3. We jumped down into the _____.

Circle the three words in each row that belong together.

4. snow rain grass hail

5. fence hill slope mountain

6. room time wall floor

7. snowman fort
   snowbank shovel

Reading Skills

1. There was no school because

   _____.

2. The girls made rooms by

   _____.

3. The girls lost track of time, so

   _____.

4. What did the girls add to their snow rooms?

   _____

   _____

5. What did Mom do when she came to get the girls?

   _____

   _____

Some of these sentences are about **real** things. Write **R** by them. The other sentences are about **make-believe** things. Write **M** by them.

6. _____ Snowflakes are magic.

7. _____ Girls make snow forts.

8. _____ Snowmen come to life.

Wilson Bentley (1865–1931)

Read about the man who taught us about snowflakes.

1   You've heard the saying that "no two snowflakes are alike." How does anyone know this? We know because of the life and work of a quiet Vermont farmer who loved snow.

2   As a boy, Wilson Bentley was interested in many things. One thing he liked to do was look at objects under a microscope. He had the idea of looking at snowflakes, and he discovered how beautiful they were, and how different.

3   As Bentley got older, he wanted to show this beauty to others. He figured out a way to take a picture through a microscope. During the next 45 years, he took pictures of more than 5,000 snowflakes. Though he never made much money, "Snowflake" Bentley was always happy to share the beauty and the mystery of snowflakes with others.

Vocabulary Skills

Fill in each blank with the right pair of letters to make a word.

ar   er   ur

1. Bentley was a quiet Vermont f_____mer.

2. He worked hard to learn how to take pict_____es.

3. He discovered that each snowflake was diff_____ent.

Circle the word in each pair that has a long vowel sound like the sound in *hope*.

4.   know   work

5.   snow   look

6.   discover   microscope

Reading Skills

Circle the word or phrase that means the same as the underlined part of each sentence.

1. Bentley <u>discovered</u> that each snowflake is different.

   found out   wondered

2. Even as a boy, Bentley was <u>interested</u> in many things.

   curious about   knew about

3. What did Bentley do when he wasn't looking at snowflakes?

   _____

   _____

4. How did Bentley get a good look at snowflakes?

   _____

   _____

5. What is one challenge that Bentley met?

   _____

   _____

6. What other challenges might Bentley have met while trying to take pictures of snowflakes?

   _____

   _____

NAME _____

Meal Mix-Up

Have you ever had a mix-up at a restaurant?

1   "All right, I think I have everything." Our server had made all of us say our orders two times. Now, it didn't seem as if he knew what to do.

2   Dad nodded, "Thanks very much." We began to talk among ourselves, so the server left.

3   We waited. We played word games. We listened to our stomachs growl.

4   At last, our server appeared with a huge tray. We watched silently as he set our plates down. Then, he left.

5   We didn't know what to do. It wasn't our food. Well, it was, but it wasn't. My green beans were in front of me, but my spaghetti was on my brother's plate. Dad's chicken was on Mom's plate, and his corn was on a plate with Cindy's pork chop.

6   There was nothing else to do. "Please pass the spaghetti," I said.

7   Everyone laughed. We passed and ate, just like we do at home.

Vocabulary Skills

Write the words from the story that have these meanings.

1. lowered and raised the head

_____
(Par. 2)

2. a low, rumbling noise

_____
(Par. 3)

3. without noise

_____
(Par. 4)

4. to hand something to someone

_____
(Par. 6)

Circle the best word for each sentence. Then, write it in the blank.

5. The chicken and the pork _____ were mixed up.

charts   chins   chops

6. We had hoped for only a _____ wait.

shape   short   shell

A word part that makes one sound is a **syllable**. Words, like *server*, that have two consonants between two vowels, are divided between the consonants: *ser / ver*. Draw a line to divide each word below into syllables.

7. o r d e r

8. n o d d e d

Reading Skills

1. This story is mostly about

_____ a rude table server.

_____ a family's mixed-up meal.

_____ a bad meal at a restaurant.

2. Number the sentences to show what happened first, second, third, and last.

_____ The family passed the food.

_____ The family waited.

_____ The server brought the food.

_____ The server took their orders.

Waiting Tables

Do you think you would like to be a server in a restaurant?

1   Almost everyone has been unhappy in a restaurant at some time or other. Sometimes, it seems as if the server can't get anything right.

2   Like any job, being a server is hard. There are many, many things to remember. First, servers have to know everything on the menu. They also have to know if anything on the menu can be changed. For example, a customer might ask, "Can I have the roast beef and mashed potatoes without the gravy?"

3   In general, servers have to keep all of their customers happy at all times. And on top of it all, servers are on their feet almost the whole time they are at work.

4   The next time you are in a restaurant, think about the hard work your server is doing. Then, remember to say "thank you."

Vocabulary Skills

Each of these words has an ending. Underline the base words.

1. seems

2. changed

3. server

4. doing

Write the story words that have these meanings.

5. sad

_____
(Par. 1)

6. keep in mind

_____
(Par. 2)

7. list of foods

_____
(Par. 2)

8. a person who buys something

_____
(Par. 3)

9. a person who waits on others

_____
(Par. 3)

Reading Skills

1. This article is mostly about

_____ what a server has to do.

_____ why servers get mixed up.

_____ how to act in a restaurant.

2. Name two things that might be hard about being a server. Write why.

_____

_____

3. If you were a server, what kind of restaurant would you want to work in? Write why.

_____

_____

Study Skills

Number the words to show A-B-C order.

4. _____ remember
   _____ job
   _____ server
   _____ restaurant

Game Night

Read to see how the game turns out.

1   Friday night is family game night at the Turners' house. Each week, a different family member chooses the game. This week, it was Cody's turn to choose. He chose his favorite board game, as always.

2   It was thundering outside, but no one minded. They were having a good time with their game. About halfway through, just as Cody was about to make a big move, everything stopped. The lights went out!

3   Everyone was silent for a few moments, then they all started talking at once. Mom felt her way to a drawer and got some candles. Dad felt his way to the fireplace for some matches.

4   Cody made his big move, by candlelight, and went on to win the game. Everybody thought this made the game even more fun. In fact, they plan to play by candlelight next week, too.

NAME _____

Vocabulary Skills

To show more than one, add **s**. If a word ends in **ch**, add **es**. So, one *inch* becomes two *inches*. Change the endings of these words to show that there are more than one.

1. one match
   two_____

2. one candle
   two_____

3. one game
   two_____

4. one watch
   two_____

Write the word from the story that is the opposite of each word.

5. same _____
   (Par. 1)

6. nothing _____
   (Par. 2)

7. noisy _____
   (Par. 3)

8. lose _____
   (Par. 4)

Reading Skills

1. How did everyone act when the lights went out?

   At first, _____

   _____

   Then, _____

   _____

   Finally, _____

   _____

2. Before the lights went out, how did you think the story would turn out?

   _____

   _____

3. Did the story turn out how you expected it to? Explain.

   _____

   _____

4. How do you think that playing by candlelight was different from playing before the lights went out?

   _____

   _____

Spectrum Reading Grade 2

149

Before There Were Lights

How did people light their homes before electricity?

1   Have you ever thought of making a lamp out of a hollow stone? That's what people did as much as 15,000 years ago. In the hollow part of the stone, they probably put some animal fat. A part of a plant lying in the fat was the wick. Scientists have also found other early lamps made out of shells and animal horns. In time, people shaped lamps out of clay.

2   About 3,000 years ago, someone came up with the idea of shaping animal fat to make candles. Because they were made of animal fat, they were smoky and smelly.

3   Even 200 years ago, candles and oil lamps were the only sources of light. Most people worked during daylight hours and went to bed when it was dark. Candles and lamp oil cost a lot of money, so people used them as little as possible.

Vocabulary Skills

Circle the best word for each sentence. Then, write it in the blank.

1. Have you ever seen an old oil _____?

   lamp   step   bump

2. A _____ is part of almost all lamps.

   tack   chunk   wick

3. People used animal _____ to make lamps for thousands of years.

   part   fat   hut

Write a word from the story that stands for this pair of words.

4. that is _____

Now, make a contraction from each pair of words.

5. should not _____

6. he has _____

7. she would _____

8. it will _____

Reading Skills

1. How could someone make a lamp out of a hollow stone?

   _____

   _____

2. What else might you have used to make a lamp a very long time ago?

   _____ an animal horn

   _____ a plastic dish

   _____ a leaf

3. Find the oldest lamp shown on the opposite page. What is it made out of? Write how you think it works.

   _____

   _____

4. Look at the second photo. How is this lamp different from the lamp in the first picture?

   _____

   _____

Answer Key

Page 3

Vocabulary Skills

Write the words from the story that have these meanings.

1. jumpy

   <u>nervous</u>
   (Par. 1)

2. very, very good

   <u>excellent</u>
   (Par. 3)

3. to repeat an action

   <u>practice</u>
   (Par. 4)

Reading Skills

1. What kinds of bridges does Dad build?

   <u>heavy, strong ones and light ones</u>

2. Why is Dad nervous?

   <u>It is his first day at a new job.</u>

3. How does the boy know that Dad is nervous?

   <u>He almost poured milk in his juice.</u>

4. What kind of bridge did the boy and Dad make at home?

   <u>They filled the boy's room with bridges</u> from boxes, blocks, and pans.

3

Page 5

Vocabulary Skills

Add **s** to a word to show more than one.

1. one bridge

   two <u>bridges</u>

2. one beam

   two <u>beams</u>

3. one cable

   many <u>cables</u>

4. one year

   eight <u>years</u>

Circle the best word for each sentence. Then, write it in the blank.

5. A bridge's supports might be called its <u>legs</u>.

   arms (legs) eyes

6. A bridge with curves underneath has <u>arches</u>.

   (arches) cables beams

Reading Skills

1. This passage is mostly about

   _____ old bridges.

   _X_ kinds of bridges.

   _____ making bridges.

2. The author wrote this selection to

   _____ make you laugh.

   _X_ help you learn.

3. Think about what you already know about bridges. What are bridges for?

   <u>to get across or to get over something; to carry things across</u>

4. This passage tells about another use for bridges. What is it?

   <u>Some bridges were made to carry water.</u>

5

Page 7

Vocabulary Skills

The words *walked, walks,* and *walking* all have the same base word, *walk*. Write the base word for each set of words below.

1. looks, looked, looking

   <u>look</u>

2. crossing, crossed, crosses

   <u>cross</u>

3. driven, drives, driving

   <u>drive</u>

4. carries, carried, carrying

   <u>carry</u>

Reading Skills

1. How does the text help you understand how long a 24-mile-long bridge is?

   <u>It takes half an hour to go across.</u>

2. How does the text help you understand how high the bridge in Colorado is?

   <u>It says that a 75-story building could fit under the bridge.</u>

3. If you do not like to look over the side of a bridge, why would the bridge in Australia be a good one to cross?

   <u>because it is very wide</u>

4. Why is the bridge in India a bridge to remember?

   <u>It is a very busy bridge, with both cars and trucks and walking traffic.</u>

7

Page 9

Vocabulary Skills

The missing word in each sentence ends with an **s**. Write the correct word in the blank.

1. The movers carried many heavy brown <u>boxes</u>.

2. Emily made <u>holes</u> in one box.

3. Emily thought her stuffed <u>animals</u> might need air.

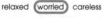

Reading Skills

1. What do Mom and Emily worry about?

   <u>They worry that their stuff will be squished.</u>

2. Circle the word that best tells how Emily feels about her stuffed animals.

   hopeless (caring) harsh

3. What word best tells how Mom feels? Circle it.

   relaxed (worried) careless

4. How do you think Dad feels about moving day?

   <u>Dad seems kind of excited.</u>

5. What clues in the story help you know how Dad feels?

   <u>He says it has been a "good day's work."</u>

9

Answer Key

Vocabulary Skills

The meanings of *new* and *old* are opposite. Make a line from each word in the first list to a word in the second list with the opposite meaning.

1. unhappy — frown
2. on — summer
3. winter — glad
4. smile — off

(lines crossing to show: unhappy→glad, on→off, winter→summer, smile→frown)

Reading Skills

1. Why was Emily happy to go turn on the lights?

   She wanted to check
   out the new house.

2. How did the picture make Emily feel?

   It made her feel
   good, even though she
   missed her old house.

3. How did Emily feel about her new house?

   She seems a little sad.
   Maybe she doesn't
   feel at home yet.

4. Write 1, 2, and 3 by these sentences to show what happened first, next, and last.

   _1_ Emily turned on the lights.

   _3_ Mom and Emily put a picture on the refrigerator.

   _2_ Mom and Emily unpacked a box.

11

Vocabulary Skills

Circle the three words in each line that belong together.

1. (green) book (white) (blue)
2. (skip) (walk) (run) shoe
3. tree (bed) (pillow) (lamp)
4. (big) top (small) (medium)

Circle the best word for each sentence. Then, write it in the blank.

5. Emily's new room is
   plain.

   pink   park   (plain)

6. Emily put her _books_ on a shelf.

   bed   (books)   boxes

7. Emily's mom put a
   quilt on the bed.

   quick   (quilt)   quiet

Reading Skills

1. This story is mostly about

   _X_ Emily's new room.

   _____ how busy Mom is.

   _____ Emily's toys.

2. At the beginning of the story, what does Emily think about her new room?

   She doesn't like it. It
   is just plain white.

3. What does Emily think of her room at the end of the story?

   She thinks it is just
   right.

4. What happened to change Emily's feelings?

   She put her books in
   place and Mom made
   her bed.

13

Vocabulary Skills

Sometimes a shorter word is used to stand for two other words. Write the shorter word from the box that stands for the underlined words in each sentence.

don't	let's
won't	we'll

1. <u>Let us</u> get ready to go.
   let's

2. We <u>will not</u> unpack today.
   won't

3. I think <u>we will</u> have a good time.
   _we'll_

4. We <u>do not</u> want to miss the taxi.
   don't

Write the story words that have these meanings.

5. worn out
   tired
   (Par. 1)

6. town
   city
   (Par. 4)

7. to begin
   start
   (Par. 6)

8. a flowing body of water
   river
   (Par. 8)

Reading Skills

Look at each picture and circle the sentence that goes with it.

1. (Emily is eating breakfast.)
   Emily is making her bed.

2. Dad is carrying a box.
   (Dad is unpacking a box.)

3. What meal is the family eating?
   breakfast

4. Why can't the family leave right away?
   Emily is not dressed yet

15

Vocabulary Skills

Circle the best word for each sentence. Then, write it in the blank.

1. Texas is a large
   state.

   start   salt   (state)

2. Grapefruit is a large yellow
   fruit.

   frame   (fruit)   flow

3. Have you seen a grapefruit
   growing?

   grab   (growing)   green

4. Oil is _drilled_ from the ground.

   (drilled)   drink   droop

Reading Skills

1. What did you know about Texas?
   Answers will vary.

2. List two new things you learned about Texas.
   Answers will vary.

3. What question would you like to ask about Texas?
   Answers will vary.

4. Why do you think the author wrote this article about Texas?

   _X_ to help me learn something

   _____ to make me laugh

Study Skills

A **heading** is a short title that gives a clue about something that comes next.

1. Under what heading might you find the size of Texas?
   How Big Is Texas?

2. Under what heading might you find the age of Texas?
   How Old Is Texas?

17

Spectrum Reading Grade 2

Answer Key

153

Answer Key

Page 19

Vocabulary Skills

Read each sentence and circle the word that is made of two shorter words. Write the two words on the lines.

1. To go up, use a (stairway.)
   __stair__   __way__

2. It's fun to ride a (streetcar.)
   __street__   __car__

3. The river runs through (downtown.)
   __down__   __town__

Reading Skills

Write each word in the correct blank.

city	concert
hotels	ride

1. If you like music, go to a __concert__.

2. San Antonio is a large, modern __city__.

3. If you are tired, __ride__ in a river taxi.

4. People sleep in __hotels__ along the River Walk.

Study Skills

Write each set of words in A-B-C order.

1. many   visit   stand
   __many__
   __stand__
   __visit__

2. place   grow   flows
   __flows__
   __grows__
   __place__

3. like   taxi   from
   __from__
   __like__
   __taxi__

Page 21

Vocabulary Skills

Circle the word in each pair that has a short vowel sound like the sound in *tip* or *jam*.

1. state   (sad)
2. (pin)   pine
3. made   (mad)
4. (hill)   hole
5. (bat)   boat

Write the story words that have these meanings.

6. mad
   __angry__ (Par. 1)

7. went up
   __climbed__ (Par. 1)

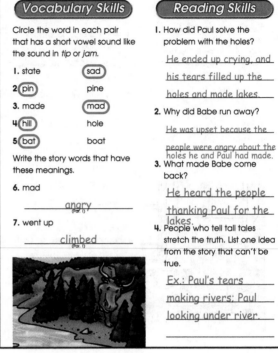

Reading Skills

1. How did Paul solve the problem with the holes?
   __He ended up crying, and his tears filled up the holes and made lakes.__

2. Why did Babe run away?
   __He was upset because the people were angry about the holes he and Paul had made.__

3. What made Babe come back?
   __He heard the people thanking Paul for the lakes.__

4. People who tell tall tales stretch the truth. List one idea from the story that can't be true.
   __Ex.: Paul's tears making rivers; Paul looking under river.__

Page 23

Vocabulary Skills

Circle the best word for each sentence. Then, write it in the blank.

1. Matt uses __green__ for his turtle.
   blue   (green)   brown

2. Mom wants to remember Gram's __flowers__.
   (flowers)   cheese   trees

3. Matt and Mom enjoy __drawing__.
   brushes   (drawing)   train

Each of these words has an ending. Underline the base words.

4. handed
5. drawing
6. trees
7. trying
8. helps
9. working
10. filled

Reading Skills

1. This story is mostly about
   _____ how to draw.
   _X_ Matt and Mom drawing.
   _____ choosing colors.

Words such as *he, she, I, this,* and *them* take the place of other words. Read these story sentences. Then, fill in the blanks.

2. "May I have the green, please?" asked Matt.
   I stands for __Matt__.

3. "Sure," said Mom. She handed it over.
   She stands for __Mom__.

4. "Drawing pretty flowers helps me remember them when the flowers are all gone."
   Them stands for __flowers__.

Circle the best answer.

5. What do you think Mom and Matt will do next?
   get ready for bed
   go to school
   (have a snack)

Page 25

Vocabulary Skills

Put a check mark by the meaning that fits the underlined word in each sentence.

1. It might be a building, a picture on a poster, or a shape in the <u>sand</u>.
   _✓_ tiny bits of dirt
   _____ to make wood smooth

2. It <u>might</u> make us ask questions, or it might make us laugh.
   _____ strength
   _✓_ maybe

Circle the word in each pair that has a long vowel sound like the sound in *case* or *fine*.

3. simple   (size)
4. (shape)   sharp
5. past   (place)
6. (take)   tack

Reading Skills

Look at each picture and circle the sentence that goes with it.

1. The blue vase is broken.
   (The vase is round and tall.)

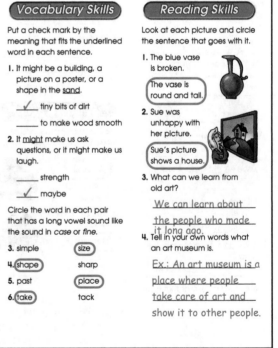

2. Sue was unhappy with her picture.
   (Sue's picture shows a house.)

3. What can we learn from old art?
   __We can learn about the people who made it long ago.__

4. Tell in your own words what an art museum is.
   __Ex.: An art museum is a place where people take care of art and show it to other people.__

Answer Key

Page 27

Vocabulary Skills

Write the story words that have these meanings.

1. uneasy, upset

   nervous
   (Par. 1)

2. a married woman

   wife
   (Par. 2)

3. trouble

   problem
   (Par. 3)

4. twelve months

   year
   (Par. 6)

Circle the three words in each line that belong together.

5. (plate) (fork) (meal) rug

6. (wife) clerk (sister) (uncle)

7. red (said) (cried) (called)

8. (chick) dog (kitten) (puppy)

9. (spring) Tuesday (summer) (winter)

Reading Skills

1. Why does Carly's face turn red the first time?

   She drops her fork; Mr. Mendez is beside her.

2. Why couldn't Mrs. Mendez come to dinner?

   She had to stay at work.

3. Why does Carly's face turn red the second time?

   Carly speaks out a little too loudly at the table.

Circle the best answer.

4. What do you think will happen next?

   Mrs. Mendez will arrive.

   (Carly will ask for a kitten.)

   Carly's cat will enter the room.

27

Page 29

Vocabulary Skills

Circle the best word for each sentence. Then, write it in the blank.

1. A pet needs a good

   home .

   roam (home) fame

2. Carly really wants a

   pet .

   (pet) meat boat

3. Mom will   wash   the dishes.

   cash (wash) fish

4. Dad will   dry   the dishes.

   (dry) why cry

The missing word in each sentence sounds like *head*. Change the first letter in *head* to **br**, **l**, or **thr**. Fill in the blanks.

5. I love the smell of fresh

   bread .

6. My spool of   thread   is empty.

7. I just broke my pencil

   lead .

Reading Skills

1. This story is mostly about

   _____ cats and dogs as pets.

   X a girl who wants a kitten.

   _____ doing chores at home.

2. Carly thinks getting a cat is a good idea. What reasons does she give?

   The animal shelter has too many; the Hamlins have one in their apartment.

3. What reason does Mom give for not getting a pet?

   The apartment is too small.

4. What would you do if you were Carly?

   Ex.: I would tell my parents I could take care of a cat all by myself.

29

Page 31

Vocabulary Skills

Read each sentence and circle the word that is made of two shorter words. Write the two words on the lines.

1. I saw cats (everywhere)

   every   where

2. (Everyone) showed respect for them.

   every   one

3. They would shave their (eyebrows.)

   eye   brows

Circle the best word for each sentence. Then, write the word in the blank.

4. In Egypt, people took   good   care of cats.

   (good) goof goal

5. They stored   grain   in huge buildings.

   (grain) grim great

6. The cats took care of the   rats   and mice.

   real rain (rats)

Reading Skills

1. The author wrote "Cats Long Ago" mostly to

   X give information.

   _____ make you laugh.

2. Compare what you know about cats in Egypt with what you know about cats today. One idea is written in for you.

   In Egypt

   cats were respected
   cats ate mice and rats
   family shaved eyebrows when a cat died

   Today

   cats are usually well cared for
   cats eat mice and rats sometimes
   family may be sad when a cat dies

3. What is one difference between us and the people in Egypt long ago?

   Ex.: Many people like cats, but we don't really respect them.

31

Page 33

Vocabulary Skills

Find a word in the story whose meaning is the same as these words.

1. grown up

   adult
   (Par. 2)

2. new, not stale

   fresh
   (Par. 3)

3. in a house

   indoors
   (Par. 4)

4. nearly

   almost
   (Par. 4)

Add **s** at the end of a word to show that there is more than one. Write these words so that they mean more than one.

5. cat   cats

6. day   days

7. week   weeks

8. pet   pets

Reading Skills

1. This article is mostly about

   _____ cats in animal shelters.

   _____ how cute kittens are.

   X daily cat care.

2. After reading the article, do you think you could care for a cat? Why or why not?

   Ex.: I think I could because I would feed and water it every day.

Study Skills

1. Write one idea that you find under each heading.

   Food

   Ex.: Fill dish once a day.

   Water

   Ex.: Give fresh water twice a day.

   Other Needs

   Ex.: Clean litter box almost every day.

2. Why do you think the author used headings in this article?

   Ex.: The headings make it easy to find information.

33

Answer Key

Vocabulary Skills

The missing words in these sentences contain the letters **oa**. Fill in the blanks.

1. Brush a cat's ___coat___ to keep it shiny.

2. Under the chin is the ___throat___.

3. For a bath, use mild ___soap___.

Read these words and look at the pictures.

the cat's bed   Tasha's cat

Add **'s** to show that something belongs to something else or someone. Show that these pets belong to their owners.

4. Mel has a cat.

   It is Mel___'s___ cat.

5. Cal has a rabbit.

   It is Cal___'s___ rabbit.

6. Shawna has a dog.

   It is Shawna___'s___ dog.

Reading Skills

1. What do cats do for themselves?

   ___They bathe___
   ___themselves several___
   ___times a day.___

2. What should a cat owner do once a year?

   ___Take the cat to the___
   ___vet___

3. Why might a long-haired cat need to be brushed more often than a short-haired cat?

   ___It would take more___
   ___work to keep the coat___
   ___neat and clean.___

4. If you had a cat, would you rather have a short-haired cat or a long-haired cat? Write why.

   ___Answers will vary.___

35

Vocabulary Skills

Circle the best word for each sentence. Then, write it in the blank.

1. Carly has high ___hopes___.

   hello   hill   (hopes)

2. Carly ___thinks___ her dad will say "no."

   (thinks)   then   throw

3. Mitch also ___wants___ to have a cat.

   went   woke   (wants)

The missing word in each sentence sounds like *kite*. Change the **k** in *kite* to **b**, **wh**, or **wr**. Fill in the blanks.

4. An unfriendly cat might ___bite___.

5. I will ___write___ and tell you about my cat.

6. Snowball is a ___white___ cat, of course.

Study Skills

Write each set of words in A-B-C order.

1. something   kitchen   please

   ___kitchen___
   ___please___
   ___something___

2. table   news   first

   ___first___
   ___news___
   ___table___

3. higher   kitten   idea

   ___higher___
   ___idea___
   ___kitten___

37

Vocabulary Skills

Write the story words that have these meanings.

1. animal kept at home

   ___pet___ (Par. 1)

2. less hard

   ___easier___ (Par. 2)

3. made a snake-like sound

   ___hiss___ (Par. 3)

4. brushed against

   ___rubbed___ (Par. 4)

Put a check mark by the meaning that fits the underlined word in each sentence.

5. One _wave_ soaked me to the skin.

   _____ to move the hand back and forth

   ___✓___ movement on the surface of a lake or ocean

6. For lunch today, I had an _orange_.

   ___✓___ a fruit

   _____ a color

Reading Skills

1. This story is mostly about

   ___X___ choosing a cat.

   _____ Mr. Mendez's work.

   _____ kittens who need homes.

2. Why didn't Carly choose the big black cat?

   ___It hissed and batted___
   ___at her hand; it wasn't___
   ___friendly___

3. How did Mitch and Carly choose the gray cat?

   ___It was friendly; it___
   ___rubbed against their___
   ___ankles.___

39

Vocabulary Skills

Read each sentence and circle the word that is made of two shorter words. Write the two words on the lines.

1. Mom was reading the (newspaper.)

   ___news___   ___paper___

2. Mouse liked the warm (sunshine.)

   ___sun___   ___shine___

Circle the best word for each sentence. Then, write it in the blank.

3. Carly knew today was ___special___.

   space   (special)   speed

4. She found Mouse ___sleeping___ in the sun.

   (sleeping)   sliding   slipping

5. Carly was quiet so she wouldn't ___scare___ the cat.

   scarf   score   (scare)

Reading Skills

1. Which sentence best tells how Carly feels about today?

   ___X___ She is excited.

   _____ She is worried.

2. What words or ideas in the story helped you answer question 1?

   ___Ex.: She wondered___
   ___what was special; she___
   ___threw back the covers.___

3. Where did Carly and Mitch look first for Mouse?

   ___They looked under___
   ___Carly's bed___

4. In what room did Carly find Mouse?

   ___in the living room___

5. Why was Mouse sleeping there?

   ___He liked the sunshine.___

41

Answer Key

Vocabulary Skills

Each of these words has an ending. Underline the base words.

1. <u>camp</u>ing
2. <u>say</u>s
3. <u>sleep</u>s
4. <u>gett</u>ing
5. <u>leave</u>s

Write the shorter word from the box that stands for the underlined words in each sentence.

I'll	we've
you're	

6. Does Dad know when <u>you are</u> leaving?

   _____ you're _____

7. After <u>we have</u> had lunch, we will walk Sparky.

   _____ we've _____

8. Later, <u>I will</u> write a letter.

   _____ I'll _____

Reading Skills

1. Why was there a picnic on the baseball field?

   It was the last day of school.

2. Why did everyone have to dash into the school?

   because it started to rain

3. Why is Kyle's family taking care of Sparky?

   because his grandparents are on a camping trip

4. Why does Sparky leave the room when Snowy comes in?

   because he is afraid of the cat

43

Vocabulary Skills

Circle the best word for each sentence. Then, write it in the blank.

1. Kyle's grandparents were happy with their __choice__.

   (choice)   check   chart

2. How __thick__ those rock walls must be!

   third   (thick)   thing

3. Through some caves, a __spring__ flows.

   (spring)   strong   swing

The prefix **un-** means *not*. Add **un** to the beginning of these words to complete these sentences.

4. Kyle was __un__able to find Sparky.

5. Kyle hoped Sparky wasn't __un__happy.

6. Snowy scratched Sparky, but Sparky was __un__hurt.

Reading Skills

1. Where did Kyle's grandparents go on their trip?

   Mammoth Cave State Park

2. Why did they go there?

   They like to look at rocks.

3. What did you learn about Kyle's grandparents by reading their letter?

   Ex.: They like to camp; they like rocks; they like hiking; they are in good health.

45

Vocabulary Skills

Put each word in the right blank.

beneath	cave
underground	

1. One <u>underground</u> passage is very steep.

2. A huge room in the cave is __beneath__ a hill.

3. We know that humans were in the __cave__ long, long ago.

Put a check mark by the meaning that fits the underlined word in each sentence.

4. We camped in a beautiful <u>spot</u>.

   ✓ a place

   ___ a stain

5. Many people <u>fish</u> in Kentucky's lakes.

   ✓ to try to catch with bait

   ___ an animal that lives in water

Reading Skills

1. This article is mostly about

   ___ how caves are formed.

   X the sights in Mammoth Cave.

   ___ animals that live in caves.

2. What is special about Mammoth Cave?

   Ex.: It is the longest cave system in the world; it has 350 miles of passages.

3. Why might a fish that lives in a cave not have any eyes?

   Ex.: It is so dark, it wouldn't be able to see anyway.

4. If you went to Mammoth Cave, what would you most like to see? Write why.

   Answers will vary.

   _____

   _____

47

Vocabulary Skills

Circle the word in each pair that has a long vowel sound like the sound in *post* or *side*.

1. (old)   got
2. grim   (times)
3. (blow)   not
4. still   (while)

Write these words so that they mean more than one.

5. post _____ posts _____
6. house _____ houses _____
7. fence _____ fences _____
8. edge _____ edges _____
9. song _____ songs _____

Reading Skills

1. Write 1, 2, and 3 by these sentences to show what happened first, next, and last.

   _2_ Dad stirred the paint.

   _1_ Michelle got the radio.

   _3_ Dad and Michelle painted.

2. What does Michelle have to do on each post?

   Paint the front, then the edge, then the other edge.

3. Why does Michelle think she will blow up?

   Ex.: There are so many posts to paint; she is tired or bored.

4. Have you ever done a task that went on and on and on? Write about it.

   Answers will vary.

   _____

   _____

49

Answer Key

Page 51

Vocabulary Skills

Write the story words that have the same meanings as these words.

1. container

   _____jug_____ (Par. 1)

2. dampen

   _____wet_____ (Par. 3)

3. incorrect

   _____wrong_____ (Par. 3)

4. saw

   _____looked_____ (Par. 4)

In each row, circle the two words with opposite meanings.

5. jump (clean) (dirty) help

6. (left) pants sticking (right)

7. (wet) push looked (dry)

8. closely spurted (fixed) (broken)

Reading Skills

Put each word in the right blank.

water	hair	milk

1. First, Danny spilled the _____milk_____.

2. Then, he had a problem with his _____hair_____.

3. Next, he got sprayed with _____water_____.

4. What did Danny look like when he sat down in his desk?

   Ex : His hair and shirt
   were wet; his shirt
   didn't match his pants.

5. Have you ever had a mixed-up day? Write about it.

   Answers will vary.
   _____
   _____
   _____
   _____

51

Page 53

Vocabulary Skills

Write the story words that have these meanings.

1. touching lightly

   _____dabbing_____ (Par. 2)

2. a mass of land that rises above the nearby area

   _____mountain_____ (Par. 2)

3. rim

   _____edge_____ (Par. 6)

Circle the letters that complete each word. Then, write the letters in the blank.

4. Megan and Halley were ready to st__ar__t.

   ir   (ar)   or

5. The baking soda went in f__ir__st.

   er   ur   (ir)

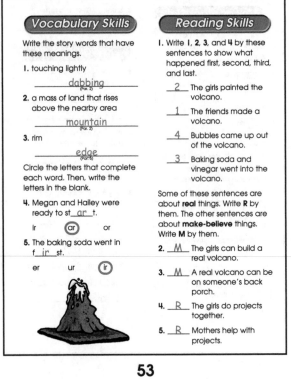

Reading Skills

1. Write 1, 2, 3, and 4 by these sentences to show what happened first, second, third, and last.

   _2_ The girls painted the volcano.

   _1_ The friends made a volcano.

   _4_ Bubbles came up out of the volcano.

   _3_ Baking soda and vinegar went into the volcano.

Some of these sentences are about **real** things. Write **R** by them. The other sentences are about **make-believe** things. Write **M** by them.

2. _M_ The girls can build a real volcano.

3. _M_ A real volcano can be on someone's back porch.

4. _R_ The girls do projects together.

5. _R_ Mothers help with projects.

53

Page 55

Vocabulary Skills

A word part that makes one sound is a **syllable**. The word *but* has one syllable. The word *button* has two syllables. Words, like *button* or *melted*, that have two consonants between two vowels, are divided between the consonants: *but / ton, mel / ted*. Draw a line to divide each word below into syllables.

1. j u m / p e r

2. u n / t i l

3. f o l / l o w

4. b a t / t e r

5. p e r / s o n

6. o r / d e r

The missing word in each sentence sounds like *sheet*. Change the **sh** in *sheet* to **f** or **gr**. Fill in the blanks.

7. Lisa was happy to _____greet_____ her cousins.

8. Mom asked us to wipe our _____feet_____.

Reading Skills

Look at each picture and circle the sentence that goes with it.

1. (Lisa's bed is neat.)
   Lisa's bed is empty.

2. (Lisa's dress is too big.)
   Lisa's dress is short.

3. What do you think will happen next?
   Lisa and her brother will go to bed.
   (The cousins will arrive soon.)
   Lisa will hide her dress-up clothes.

55

Page 57

Vocabulary Skills

Put a check mark by the meaning that fits the underlined word in each sentence.

1. Let Mom <u>watch</u> the road.

   _X_ see, look at

   ____ a machine that keeps time

2. This car seat is <u>mine</u>.

   ____ a place for digging rocks

   _X_ belongs to me

Circle the word in each pair that has a short vowel sound like the sound in *men*.

3. (yes)   seat

4. tear   (tell)

5. (spend)   eat

Reading Skills

1. How does everyone feel about going to the zoo?

   ____ They are tired.

   _X_ They are eager.

Words such as *he, she,* and *I* take the place of other words. Read these story sentences. Then, fill in the blanks.

2. "Here I come!" sang Jake from the back seat.

   I stands for _____Jake_____

3. Julia was very grown-up. "I would rather spend my time looking at animals that don't want to eat me."

   Me stands for _____Julia_____

4. "What about you, Lisa?" Mrs. Shaw asked.

   You stands for _____Lisa_____

Write each word in the correct blank.

   buckled   spend

5. The car doesn't go until everyone is _____buckled_____ in.

6. Watch how much you _____spend_____ at the zoo.

7. What animals would you like to see if you went to the zoo?

   Answers will vary.
   _____
   _____

57

Answer Key

Page 59

Look at these words. They are broken into syllables. Sound out each syllable. Then, say the words aloud.

1. antelopes
   an / te / lopes

2. wildebeest
   wil / de / beest

The missing words in these sentences contain the letters **oi**. Fill in the blanks.

3. If the herd is running, you will hear the __noise__ .

4. If I had a __choice__ , I would watch the otters.

5. I hope the rain doesn't __spoil__ our trip.

Reading Skills

1. What is a large group of zebras called?

   __a herd__

2. Why does a herd move from place to place?

   __They eat grass, then move__
   __to a new place where__
   __there is more grass.__

3. What are some other animals that move in groups?

   __antelopes, gnus,__
   __wildebeest__

4. Why do zebras' stripes make it hard for lions to catch a zebra?

   __Ex.: The stripes make__
   __the zebras blend__
   __together. The lion__
   __can't see just one__
   __zebra to chase.__

59

Page 61

Vocabulary Skills

Circle the three words in each line that belong together.

1. (river) forest (lake) (pond)
2. rock (grass) (tree) (bush)
3. (mountain) (hill) swamp (cliff)

Circle the best word for each sentence. Then, write it in the blank.

4. The lion is known as the __king__ of the beasts.

   cling (king) thing

5. You may have to __search__ all day to find a lion.

   (search) touch pitch

6. A cub stays with its __mother__ for more than two years.

   (mother) father brother

Reading Skills

1. In what three kinds of places do tigers live?

   __mountains__
   __forests__
   __wet, grassy areas__

2. How are these places different?

   __Answers will vary.__

3. How does the author help you with the word *tigress*?

   __The author wrote__
   __"mother tiger" first, then__
   __used the word "tigress."__

Study Skills

1. Under what heading can you find information about when a tiger hunts?

   __How Tigers Live__

61

Page 63

Vocabulary Skills

Some words change form when they are made plural. Draw a line from the singular form in the first column to the correct plural form in the second column.

1. one wing — two feet
2. one mouse — two wings
3. one foot — three toes
4. one toe — many mice

Write the story words that have these meanings.

5. quiet
   __silent__ (Par. 1)

6. very, very good
   __excellent__ (Par. 2)

7. having a fine point
   __sharp__ (Par. 3)

Reading Skills

Use what you know or what you just read about owls to answer these questions.

1. Would owls be able to live in a city? Explain.

   __Answers will vary.__

2. What would happen if an owl made noise as it flew?

   __Ex.: It would not be able__
   __to sneak up on its prey.__

3. This owl is asleep.

   [This owl is awake.]

Study Skills

1. What do the three headings have in common?

   __They all name parts of__
   __an owl's body.__

63

Page 65

Vocabulary Skills

Circle the best word for each sentence. Then, write it in the blank.

1. Charlie wanted to __rest__ .

   smart hear (rest)

2. Julia wanted to __sleep__ in a tree.

   (sleep) mop trap

3. Jake is still ready for __action__ .

   spin noon (action)

4. Lisa was __afraid__ to ask her question.

   shed (afraid) blend

In each row, circle the two words with opposite meanings.

5. awake (wise) (foolish) dirty
6. (weak) action (strong) tired

Reading Skills

1. Why didn't Julia care for the sleeping tiger?

   __It was lying in the__
   __dirt.__

2. Why does Lisa want stripes?

   __She wants stripes__
   __because she liked the__
   __zebras so much.__

Some of these sentences are about **real** things. Write **R** by them. The other sentences are about **make-believe** things. Write **M** by them.

3. __M__ Animals ride in car seats.
4. __R__ Children sleep in beds.
5. __R__ People climb rocks.
6. __M__ Girls perch in trees.

65

Answer Key

Page 67

Write the shorter word from the box that stands for the underlined words in each sentence.

she'd	wouldn't
wasn't	

1. Gram was not humming in the kitchen.

   _____ wasn't _____

2. If I caught her dancing, she would turn red.

   _____ she'd _____

3. Gramps would not stop telling stories.

   _____ wouldn't _____

Each of these words has an ending. Underline the base words.

4. waved
5. brothers
6. seemed
7. watched

1. Which word best describes the boy's feelings about his grandparents?

   (fond)   excited   hopeless

2. Why do you think the fort "got bigger" every time Gramps told the story?

   Ex.: He wanted to keep the story interesting, so he had to change it each time.

3. What do you think the boy might do next?

   Answers will vary. Ex.: He might build a fort with his dad.

4. Mark the sentence that is true.

   _X_ Gramps grew up on a farm.

   ____ Gramps grew up in the city.

5. What information in the story helped you answer question 4?

   Gramps and his brother had a barn with hay.

67

Page 69

Read each sentence and circle the word that is made of two shorter words. Write the two words on the lines.

1. Gina and Mom filled a rainy (afternoon.)

   __ after __   __ noon __

2. The (raindrops) told Gina that swimming was out.

   __ rain __   __ drops __

3. Was there (anything) besides kid games?

   __ any __   __ thing __

Circle the word in each pair that has a short vowel sound like the sounds in *fun* and *kid*.

4. clue   (rumble)

5. (sticks)   slide

6. (swim)   bite

1. Gina knows she will not be able to swim this afternoon because she hears thunder.

2. Mom frowned because she saw that it was raining outside.

3. This story is mostly about

   ____ the rules for playing hopscotch.

   ____ cleaning out a closet full of games.

   _X_ how a girl and her mom spend an afternoon.

4. Why didn't Gina like her mom's ideas at first?

   She thought they were little-kid games.

5. How did the afternoon turn out for Gina?

   She thought it was pretty fun, even if they were little-kid games.

69

Page 71

In each row, circle the letters in each word that make the same sound you hear in the underlined word.

h(ea)t   tr(ee)   sh(e)   l(ea)f

1. r(ai)n   p(a)per   w(ai)t   tod(ay)

2. sn(ow)   (o)dd   dr(o)ve   ech(o)

3. cl(ou)d   (ou)r   b(ow)n   h(ow)

Write the story words that have the same meanings as these words.

4. warmth _____ heat (Par. 1)

5. go up _____ rise (Par. 2)

6. comes down _____ falls (Par. 3)

1. Write 1, 2, 3, and 4 by these sentences to show the correct order of the steps in the water cycle.

   _4_ Rain, snow, hail, or sleet falls to the ground.

   _2_ Water vapor rises and forms clouds.

   _1_ The sun's heat causes water to form water vapor.

   _3_ Water drops form and become heavy.

1. Look at the picture of the water cycle. What do the arrows above the ocean tell you?

   Ex.: They show what direction the water is moving.

2. Explain the water cycle in your own words.

   Answers will vary.

   _____

   _____

   _____

71

Page 73

The prefix **re-** means *again*. Add **re** to the beginning of these words to complete these sentences.

1. Dad had to _re_ write the list.

2. Gina wanted to _re_ heat her lunch.

3. Mom had to _re_ wash the corn.

Put a check mark by the meaning that fits the underlined word in each sentence.

4. All I could think about was sinking my teeth into that corn.

   _✓_ a vegetable

   ____ a sore spot on a toe

5. I turned my ear in his direction.

   ____ a cob of corn

   _✓_ human organ related to hearing

Put each word in the right blank.

   excited   fresh   picked

1. Dad got _excited_ about the corn.

2. Have you ever _picked_ corn?

3. Some people won't eat anything but _fresh_ corn.

4. Why does Gina's dad get excited about the corn?

   because he knows it's fresh

5. Why isn't some of the fresh food really fresh?

   It may have been picked days or weeks ago, then washed and trucked in to the store.

73

Answer Key

Vocabulary Skills

Circle the word in each pair that has a short vowel sound like the sounds in *hot* and *ran*.

1. do (chop)
2. (stop) row
3. (pass) day
4. paint (plant)

Reading Skills

Write these steps in the correct order.

- watch plants grow
- plant seeds
- water soil
- harvest corn
- prepare soil

1. prepare soil
2. plant seeds
3. water soil
4. watch plants grow
5. harvest corn

Study Skills

Write each set of words in A-B-C order.

1. corn   garden   backyard
   backyard
   corn
   garden

2. soil   dirt   clumps
   clumps
   dirt
   soil

3. seeds   rows   weeds
   rows
   seeds
   weeds

4. plant   harvest   days
   days
   harvest
   plant

75

Vocabulary Skills

Circle the letters that complete each word. Then, write the letters in the blank.

1. Did you have c_or_n last week?
   ur   er   (or)

2. These muffins are sweetened with corn s_yr_up.
   (yr)   ur   ar

3. Does your laundry soap contain corn st_ar_ch?
   ir   (ar)   er

The missing words in these sentences contain the letters **ou**. Fill in the blanks.

4. The news _about_ the corn crop is good.

5. I can't name four hundred things, much less four _thousand_ things made of corn!

6. Listen to the _sound_ of the corn blowing in the wind.

Reading Skills

1. Today, corn is used in thousands of products. How is that different from many years ago?
   It used to be eaten or fed to cattle and hogs.

2. The article mentions two products that come from corn. What are they?
   corn syrup
   corn starch
   What are they used for?
   Ex.: They are used in many products, from paper to laundry soap to medicines.

3. Half of the corn grown in America is fed to cattle and hogs. Why is that important?
   Answers will vary.
   _____

77

Vocabulary Skills

Write the story words that have these meanings.

1. outdoor meal
   picnic (Par. 1)

2. not common
   unusual (Par. 1)

3. dried grapes
   raisins (Par. 2)

4. smiling widely
   grinning (Par. 6)

Circle the best word for each sentence. Then, write the word in the blank.

5. Gina was not eager to try the _salads_ at the picnic.
   salt   (salads)   sales

6. Gina was surprised to find _fruit_ on the pizza.
   fine   faint   (fruit)

Reading Skills

Words such as *she*, *you*, and *it* take the place of other words. Read these story sentences. Then, fill in the blanks.

1. "Gina, don't you want some of this salad?"
   You stands for _Gina_.

2. "Gina, try this pizza. It is great!" he said.
   It stands for _pizza_.

3. Which of these sentences best tells how Gina feels about food?
   ___ If it's food, I'll try it.
   ___ I like to try new foods.
   _X_ I'll try something only if I know what it is.
   ___ I like trying foods that have fruit in them.

4. Did Gina like the fruit pizza? How could you tell?
   She liked it. She asked for another piece, then asked for the recipe.

79

Vocabulary Skills

Recipes often use short forms of words called **abbreviations**. Match the abbreviations in the box with their common recipe words.

C.	tsp.
oz.	pkg.

1. teaspoon _tsp._
2. cup _C._
3. ounce _oz._
4. package _pkg._

Write these words so that they mean more than one.

5. ounce _ounces_
6. teaspoon _teaspoons_
7. minute _minutes_
8. tray _trays_
9. sheet _sheets_
10. circle _circles_

Reading Skills

Write these steps in the correct order. (Not all of the recipe's steps are here.)

- chill
- bake dough
- press dough into circle
- slice and arrange fruit
- make cream cheese mixture

1. press dough into circle
2. bake dough
3. make cream cheese mixture
4. slice and arrange fruit
5. chill

81

Answer Key

Page 83

Vocabulary Skills

Circle the word in each pair that has a long vowel sound like the sound in *mean* or *phone*.

1. (seen)   sent
2. bus   (bone)
3. worth   (whole)
4. getting   (green)

Add **'s** to show that something belongs to someone. Write the new words.

5. The grass belongs to Yuki.
   It is _Yuki's_ grass.
6. The house belongs to Mom.
   It is _Mom's_ house.

Reading Skills

1. This story is mostly about
   _____ a girl playing in the wet grass.
   _____ how a rain storm hurt some plants.
   _X_ two neighbor girls and how they meet.

Some words make us feel better than other words. For example, look at these sentences.

   I had some <u>mushy</u> ice cream.
   I had some <u>soft</u> ice cream.

If you're like most people, mushy ice cream doesn't sound very good to you. The word *mushy* makes us think of rotten things.

Read each sentence below. Think about the underlined words. Put a check mark next to the sentence that gives you better feelings.

2. _✓_ The grass looked <u>shiny</u>.
   _____ The grass looked <u>wet</u>.
3. _✓_ Yuki's mom <u>stepped</u> out.
   _____ Yuki's mom <u>stomped</u> out.
4. _____ The flowers were <u>skinny</u>.
   _✓_ The flowers were <u>narrow</u>.

Page 85

Vocabulary Skills

A word part that makes one sound is a **syllable**. The word *sun* has one syllable. The word *funny* has two syllables. Words, like *funny* or *halted*, that have two consonants between two vowels, are divided between the consonants: *fun / ny*, *hal / ted*. Draw a line to divide each word below into syllables.

1. g a r / d e n
2. s u n / n y
3. v i l / l a g e
4. b e r / r y

Circle the three words in each line that belong together.

5. (round) large (square) (oval)
6. (soil) (dirt) (mud) seed
7. (sunflower) bird (rose) (daisy)
8. (rake) (hoe) (shovel) bush

Reading Skills

1. What did you think of when you read the title, "The Sunflower House"?
   Answers will vary.

2. Was your idea anything like the sunflower house described in the directions? Explain.
   Answers will vary.

Study Skills

1. What information is given only in the diagram?
   The measurements of the circle and the ditch.

2. Would you have been able to follow the directions without the diagram? Explain.
   Answers will vary.

Page 87

Vocabulary Skills

The missing word in each sentence sounds like *match*. Change the **m** in *match* to **c**, **l**, or **p**. Fill in the blanks.

1. I watered the _patch_ of new grass.
2. Remember to close the _latch_.
3. He didn't make the _catch_.

Circle the best word for each sentence. Then, write it in the blank.

4. The game began with, "Let's _play_ ball!"
   (play)   plow   plain
5. The batter _swung_ at the ball.
   sled   slowed   (swung)
6. The game was a _dream_ come true.
   (dream)   drew   dress

Reading Skills

1. Why is David's grandfather afraid?
   He feels bad about
   their seats.

2. How does David feel about the seats at first, and then later?
   He doesn't really care
   at first. Later he says
   they were great seats.

3. What three things does David remember?
   players on green grass
   smell of popcorn
   smack of ball in mitt

4. What sights, smells, and sounds do you remember from a special day?
   Answers will vary.

Page 89

Vocabulary Skills

Write the words from the story that have these meanings.

1. sections of a baseball game
   inning
   (Par. 2)
2. a group of people
   team
   (Par. 3)
3. springs back
   bounces
   (Par. 4)

Circle the word that is the opposite of the underlined word.

4. <u>enjoy</u> (dislike) choose   hope
5. <u>lose</u> hit (win) turn
6. <u>run</u> tag (walk) trade

Reading Skills

1. What did you learn about baseball after you read this article?
   Answers will vary.

2. What happens during an inning?
   Each team gets a turn
   to bat and to field.

3. What can a runner do to be safe?
   stop at first, second,
   or third base.

4. Why do you think the author wrote this article?
   _X_ to give information
   _____ to entertain

Answer Key

Page 91

Check the meaning that fits the underlined word in each sentence.

1. The fans took their seats.

___ machines that blow air

✓ people who support a team

2. He had ten sets of cards.

✓ groups that fit together

___ parts of a tennis match

Circle the best word for each sentence. Then, write it in the blank.

3. We waited eagerly for the first __pitch__.

inch (pitch) branch

4. I would be afraid to __swing__ and miss!

(swing) bring fling

5. I slept through the __ninth__ inning.

(ninth) truth cloth

Reading Skills

Put each word in the right blank.

| adults | collect | rare |

1. How much is a __rare__ card worth?

2. Only __adults__ could pay that much!

3. Many people like to __collect__ cards.

4. This article is mostly about

___ the greatest baseball teams.

___ the history of baseball.

_X_ collecting baseball cards.

5. Do you collect anything? Write about it.

__Answers will vary.__

91

Page 93

Vocabulary Skills

Circle the best word for each sentence. Then, write it in the blank.

1. Great-grandmother Lucy had white __hair__.

pair flair (hair)

2. She wore a __dress__.

class (dress) miss

3. Lorna didn't understand about the __house__.

blouse (house) mouse

Each of these words has an ending. Underline the base words.

4. pointed

5. closely

6. wearing

7. houses

Reading Skills

Some of these sentences are about **real** things. Write **R** by them. The other sentences are about **make-believe** things. Write **M** by them.

1. _M_ Houses are not on the ground.

2. _M_ Children wear space suits.

3. _R_ People look at old pictures.

4. What do you learn about Lorna from the picture?

__Ex.: Her house looks like a space ship. It is high off the ground.__

5. Why does Lorna ask about getting a car up to a house?

__Ex.: Her house is up off the ground, so she thinks houses always were that way.__

6. Look at the picture. What do you like best about Lorna's world?

__Answers will vary.__

93

Page 95

Vocabulary Skills

Write the story words that have the same meanings as these words.

1. entire

__whole__ (Par. 1)

2. good-tasting

__yummy__ (Par. 2)

3. unwell

__sick__ (Par. 2)

4. new

__fresh__ (Par. 4)

Write a word from the story that stands for each pair of words.

5. I will __I'll__

6. it is __it's__

Reading Skills

Write one thing you know about each of Rachel's neighbors.

1. Mr. and Mrs. Rotollo

__Italian, helped make dinner__

2. Philip

__dancer, lives above Rachel, wakes her up__

3. Mr. Tran

__runs grocery, gives Rachel best food__

4. Mrs. Moya

__runs shop, takes down piñatas when it rains__

5. Look at the picture and the story. Which neighbor seems most interesting to you? Write why.

__Answers will vary.__

95

Page 97

Vocabulary Skills

Write the words from the article that have these meanings.

1. garbage

__trash__ (Par. 1)

2. places to eat

__restaurants__ (Par. 2)

3. go along with

__agree__ (Par. 3)

The missing words in these sentences contain the letters **oa**. Fill in the blanks.

4. The mayor rode a __float__ in the parade.

5. The street is lined with __oak__ trees.

6. Even the plow could not get up our icy __road__.

7. We take our __boat__ to the lake.

Reading Skills

1. This article is mostly about

_X_ what makes a city.

___ how to live in a city.

___ America's largest cities.

2. What is your favorite thing to do in your city or in a nearby city? Write about it.

__Answers will vary.__

3. The person who wrote this article is the __author__.

4. Do you think this article is meant to give information or to make you laugh? Write why.

__To give information; reasons will vary.__

97

Answer Key

Page 99

Vocabulary Skills

Read each sentence and circle the word that is made of two shorter words. Write the two words on the lines.

1. In the story, who had (nowhere) to go in winter?

   ___no___   ___where___

2. Ant talked to (himself) as he worked.

   ___him___   ___self___

3. (Grasshopper) did not get ready for winter.

   ___grass___   ___hopper___

The word ending **-est** means *most*, as in *luckiest*. Add **est** to each underlined word to change its meaning.

4. Ant was <u>smart</u>. ___smartest___

5. Mole was <u>soft</u>. ___softest___

6. Grasshopper could jump <u>high</u>. ___highest___

Reading Skills

Some of these sentences are about **real** things. Write **R** by them. The other sentences are about **make-believe** things. Write **M** by them.

1. __R__ Ants gather food.

2. __M__ Grasshoppers watch baseball games.

3. __M__ Grasshoppers are lazy.

4. This story is called a **fable**. Fables usually teach a lesson. What lesson does this one teach?

   Ex.: It is good to plan ahead; store food for the winter.

5. If you were Ant, what would you have said to Grasshopper?

   Answers will vary.

99

Page 101

Vocabulary Skills

Circle the word that has a short vowel sound like the one in the underlined word.

1. <u>king</u>   smiled   (silly)

2. <u>castle</u>   waved   (happy)

3. <u>met</u>   (dress)   few

4. <u>sad</u>   day   (mad)

Reading Skills

1. How did the princess feel when she waved and no one waved back?

   It made her mad and sad.

2. How did the princess speak to the market girl?

   _____ She spoke pleasantly.

   __X__ She spoke angrily.

   _____ She begged her.

3. What lesson did the princess learn from the market girl?

   If she is pleasant, others will be pleasant to her.

Number the words to show A-B-C order for each list.

4. __2__ pleasant

   __4__ wave

   __1__ market

   __3__ sad

5. __4__ smile

   __3__ princess

   __1__ castle

   __2__ happy

101

Page 103

Vocabulary Skills

Look at these words. They are broken into syllables. Sound out each syllable. Then, say the words aloud.

1. protection   pro / tec / tion

2. enemies   e / ne / mies

The word ending **-er** means *more*. So, *higher* means *more high*. Add **er** to each underlined word to change its meaning.

3. Our castle wall is <u>thick</u>.

   ___thicker___

4. Their castle wall is <u>tall</u>.

   ___taller___

5. His castle wall is <u>strong</u>.

   ___stronger___

Reading Skills

1. How are castles different from our homes? List some ways.

Castles

Walls <u>Tall, thick, strong;</u> <u>usually made of stone.</u>

Purpose <u>For protection and</u> <u>for shelter from weather</u>

Our Homes

Walls <u>Usually one or two</u> <u>stories high; made of wood.</u>

Purpose <u>For shelter from</u> <u>weather</u>

2. Imagine that you are standing on the wall of the castle shown on page 102. Describe what you see.

   Answers will vary.

103

Page 105

Vocabulary Skills

The missing word in each sentence sounds like *sale*. Change the **s** in *sale* to **g, p,** or **t**. Fill in the blanks.

1. The story made quite a ___tale___ to tell.

2. The strong wind might have been a ___gale___.

3. If you are afraid, you might be ___pale___.

Reading Skills

1. What two things made this yard sale day a time to remember?

   <u>the wind storm</u>

   <u>the helpful neighbors</u>

2. In the story, there is a problem. What is the problem and how is it solved?

   Problem <u>The wind storm</u> <u>messes up the sale.</u>

How it is solved <u>The</u> <u>neighbors help clean up.</u>

3. Write **1, 2, 3,** and **4** by these sentences to show the correct order from the story.

   __2__ People began coming to the sale.

   __4__ Neighbors came to help.

   __3__ The storm blew through.

   __1__ The family set things out on tables.

4. The person who tells a story is the **narrator**. What did the narrator like best about the yard sale day?

   <u>The narrator liked the</u> <u>time spent with the</u> <u>neighbors best.</u>

105

Answer Key

Page 107

Vocabulary Skills

Circle the best word for each sentence. Then, write the word in the blank.

1. The students were busy making ___flowers___ .

   (flowers) flakes flutes

2. Greg asked for more ___pipe___ cleaners.

   point part (pipe)

3. No one even heard the ___bell___ ring.

   bark bowl (bell)

Add **'s** to show that something belongs to someone. Write the new words.

4. The desk belongs to Mrs. Davis.

   It is Mrs. ___Davis's___ desk.

5. The flower belongs to Greg.

   It is ___Greg's___ flower.

6. The idea belongs to Caitlyn.

   It is ___Caitlyn's___ idea.

Reading Skills

1. Circle the word that best tells about Caitlyn.

   selfish (thoughtful) careless

2. Circle the word that best tells about Mrs. Davis.

   (nice) nervous angry

3. What parts of the story helped you learn about Mrs. Davis?

   Answers will vary. Ex.: She is

   helpful. She doesn't stop the
   students from working.

Study Skills

Number the words to show A-B-C order for each list.

1. __1__ desk
   __4__ students
   __3__ room
   __2__ flowers

2. __2__ idea
   __3__ parents
   __1__ hand
   __4__ working

107

Page 109

Vocabulary Skills

To show more than one, add **s**. If a word ends in **y**, change the **y** to **i** and add **es**. So, *one fly* becomes *two flies*. Change the endings of these words to show that there are more than one.

1. one butterfly
   two ___butterflies___

2. one lady
   two ___ladies___

3. one city
   two ___cities___

Circle the best word for each sentence. Then, write it in the blank.

4. Unlike real flowers, fake flowers don't ___droop___ .

   draw (droop) drain

5. Jenny used ___crazy___ colors on her flower.

   (crazy) crow cream

6. Mom thought Ted's work was ___great___ .

   grass (great) grin

Reading Skills

Put each word in the right blank.

excited	model	poster

1. The butterfly ___model___ even had wings that flapped.

2. Even Mrs. Davis was ___excited___ about the Open House.

3. The picture on the ___poster___ showed a sunflower.

4. This story is mostly about

   _____ how hard Mrs. Davis worked.

   __X__ Ted and his parents at the Open House.

   _____ the parts of a butterfly.

5. Have you ever been excited about an Open House or a school project? Write about it.

   Answers will vary.
   _____
   _____
   _____

109

Page 111

Vocabulary Skills

Circle the three words in each row that belong together.

1. (water) (milk) cheese (juice)

2. (twist) drip (bend) (curl)

3. paper (center) (edge) (corner)

Reading Skills

Write these steps in the correct order. (Not all of the steps are listed here.)

- flatten coffee filter
- drip paint onto coffee filter
- let dry
- gather supplies
- wet down coffee filter

1. _gather supplies_

2. _flatten coffee filter_

3. _wet down coffee filter_

4. _drip paint onto coffee filter_

5. _let dry_

Study Skills

1. Which *Reading Skills* step does the illustration show?

   Step 4

2. How did the illustrations help you understand the project?

   Answers will vary.
   _____
   _____
   _____
   _____
   _____
   _____
   _____
   _____
   _____
   _____

111

Page 113

Vocabulary Skills

The missing words in these sentences contain the letters **ee** or **ea**. Fill in the blanks.

1. Most plants begin from ___seeds___ .

2. The biggest type of plant is a ___tree___ .

3. I don't want to rake even one more ___leaf___ .

Reading Skills

1. What jobs do a plant's leaves do?

   Leaves collect energy
   from the sun and make
   food for the plant.

2. Write what nutrients are.

   Nutrients are the
   food that the roots
   get from the soil.

3. After the roots collect water and nutrients, what happens?

   The nutrients go up
   the stem to the leaves.

Study Skills

1. The illustration on page 112 includes **call-outs**, short pieces of information that explain parts of an illustration. How can you tell what each callout is telling about?

   An arrow connects
   each callout to one
   part of the plant.

113

Answer Key

Page 115

Vocabulary Skills

Write the words from the article that have these meanings.

1. feeling tired and unhappy
   bored (Par. 1)

2. crabby
   grumpy (Par. 2)

3. dragged her feet
   shuffled (Par. 3)

Circle the word in each pair that has a long vowel sound like the sound of **a-e** in *make* or **ee** in *seem*.

5. help ⟨need⟩
6. ⟨weaving⟩ else
7. ⟨game⟩ said
8. ⟨day⟩ had

Reading Skills

1. At the beginning of the story, Allison is bored and Mom is busy. How did you think the story was going to turn out?
   Answers will vary.

2. Why can't Mom help Allison?
   She is busy making food for a neighbor who broke her leg.

3. How does Allison feel when she finds out what her mother was doing?
   She feels less grumpy.

   Why do you think she feels that way?
   Answers will vary.

Write **T** if the sentence is true. Write **N** if the story does not give the information.

4. __T__ Mom is kind to a neighbor.
   __N__ Mom dislikes playing games with Allison.
   __N__ Mom is a great cook.
   __T__ Mom uses a nickname for her daughter.

115

Page 117

Vocabulary Skills

A word part that makes one sound is a **syllable**. The word *but* has one syllable. The word *butter* has two syllables. Words, like *butter*, that have two consonants between two vowels, are divided between the consonants: *but / ter*. Draw a line to divide each word below into syllables.

1. bas/ket
2. cor/her
3. con/fuse
4. nod/ded
5. sum/mer

Circle the word that is the opposite of the underlined word.

6. outside special ⟨inside⟩ every
7. opened ⟨closed⟩ filled tossed

Reading Skills

Some words create pictures in our minds. For example, look at these sentences.

   Mark rode his bike around the block.

   Mark zoomed his bike around the block.

Rode tells you what Mark did, but *zoomed* really tells you how he did it and how he looked as he did it.

Read each sentence below. Think about the underlined words. Make a check mark next to the sentence that really tells you what the character did or how something looks.

1. _____ Mark put a can into his basket.
   __✓__ Mark tossed a can into his basket.

2. __✓__ He flashed a smile.
   _____ He smiled.

117

Page 119

Vocabulary Skills

Write the story words that have the same meanings as these words.

1. told
   explained (Par. 1)

2. thankful
   grateful (Par. 2)

3. put or throw
   dump (Par. 2)

4. act of kindness
   favor (Par. 3)

Circle the best word for each sentence. Then, write it in the blank.

5. Timo could not __think__ of a way.
   thick ⟨think⟩ thank

6. The boys __threw__ the clippings into the truck.
   thing third ⟨threw⟩

7. They ran into Mr. Timmons by __chance__.
   change ⟨chance⟩ chain

Reading Skills

1. Why did the boys take a walk?
   to think about their problem with the cans

2. Why did Mr. Timmons need help with his lawn?
   He had hurt his foot and had to use a cane.

Look at the picture. Put a check mark by the two sentences that tell about the picture.

3. _____ Mr. Timmons is asleep.
   __✓__ Mr. Timmons uses a cane.
   __✓__ Mr. Timmons is wearing jeans.

119

Page 121

Vocabulary Skills

The prefix **re-** means *again*. Add **re** to the beginning of these words to complete these sentences.

1. The boys had to __re__count their money.

2. Maybe they should __re__cycle more cans.

Circle the letters that complete each word. Then, write the letters in the blank.

3. Mark and Timo worked h__ar__d on the lawn.
   ⟨ar⟩ er ur

4. Timo could only imagine being in a hot a__ir__ balloon.
   or ⟨ir⟩ ar

5. They will certainly need m__or__e trash bags.
   ar ⟨or⟩ er

Reading Skills

1. What did the boys do yesterday?
   They took their cans to the recycling center.

2. Today, the boys are counting their money.

3. How did Mr. Timmons feel about helping the boys?
   He was glad, cheerful

4. What part of the story helped you answer question 3?
   It says he laughed when he said his truck hadn't worked so hard in a long time.

5. After Mark picked up the can, he laughed because they were done collecting cans.

6. What does "old habits die hard" mean? Do you think it is true?
   Answers will vary.

121

Answer Key

Page 123

Vocabulary Skills

Circle the best word for each sentence. Then, write it in the blank.

1. Mr. Timmons seemed __pleased__.
   (**pleased**) ended bread

2. He still needs his __cane__.
   tune shine (**cane**)

3. Mr. Timmons is glad to __help__.
   trap (**help**) drop

To show more than one, add **s** to the word. Some words don't follow that pattern, though. Use the words in the box to complete each sentence. Then, write the singular form of the word on the line after each sentence.

people	children
mice	

4. Mark saw two __mice__ in the garage. __mouse__

5. Mr. Timmons likes __children__. __child__

6. Many __people__ help at the food pantry. __person__

Reading Skills

1. This story is mostly about
   _____ how a food pantry works.
   _____ what Mr. Timmons does in his free time.
   __X__ what the boys decide to do with their money.

2. Mr. Timmons is going to
   help at the food pantry.

3. What will Mr. Timmons do there?
   He will pack or unpack cans of food.

4. Mr. Timmons says something that gives the boys an idea. What does he say?
   He says some people don't have enough money to buy food for their families.

123

Page 125

Vocabulary Skills

Circle the word that means the opposite of the underlined word.

1. empty again use (**full**)

2. save part (**waste**) buy

Write the words from the article that have these meanings.

3. one of two equal parts
   __half__ (Par. 2)

4. pay money for
   __buy__ (Par. 2)

5. power
   __energy__ (Par. 3)

6. what is thrown away
   __waste__ (Par. 4)

Reading Skills

1. This article is mostly about
   _____ cans at the grocery store.
   __X__ recycling aluminum cans.
   _____ how to recycle aluminum.

2. If you buy a can of lemonade, drink it, and recycle it, how long will it take for that can to be recycled and made into new cans?
   about 60 days

3. It makes sense to recycle because recycling saves money, and energy, and cuts down on waste

Study Skills

1. What does the graph show?
   It shows how much energy it takes to make a can out of new aluminum and out of recycled aluminum.

2. Why do you think the author included a graph with this article?
   Answers will vary.

125

Page 127

Vocabulary Skills

Each of these words has an ending. Underline the base words.

1. wanted
2. yelled
3. dashed
4. turned

For most words that end in **e**, drop the **e** before adding **ed** or **ing**. Add the endings **-ed** and **-ing** to these words. Remember to drop the **e** first. One is done for you.

scrape + ed __scraped__
scrape + ing __scraping__

5. race + ed __raced__
   race + ing __racing__

6. trade + ed __traded__
   trade + ing __trading__

Write a word from the story that stands for each pair of words.

7. I will __I'll__
8. should not __shouldn't__

Reading Skills

Choose the best word to finish each sentence below. Write the word in the blank.

1. The girls want to be the __first__ ones into the pool.
   dash (**first**) next

2. Katie slowed down when the whistle __blew__.
   (**blew**) cool walk

3. Katie hurt her elbow when she __fell__.
   feet backward (**fell**)

4. What rule do you think Katie and Sara were breaking?
   no running

5. Why do you think most pools have this rule?
   Answers will vary.

6. What else do you know about pool rules?
   Answers will vary.

127

Page 129

Vocabulary Skills

Write the words from the story that have these meanings.

1. looked carefully
   __peered__ (Par. 1)

2. most liked
   __favorite__ (Par. 1)

3. hair from sheep
   __wool__ (Par. 3)

4. an amount of heat
   __warmth__ (Par. 5)

In each sentence, circle each word that has the same vowel sound as the underlined word.

5. headed
   Ryan's favorite (**sweater**) wa(**red**)

6. Nick
   (**This**) is Ryan's friend.

7. Mom
   She thinks Ryan will get (**hot**).

8. back
   Ryan wa(**glad**) to change shirts.

Reading Skills

1. What did you think as Ryan was finding his favorite sweater? Did it seem like a good idea?
   Answers will vary.

2. Are there any clues in the picture that tell you it is a hot day? What are they?
   Answers will vary.

3. What causes Mom to raise her eyebrow?
   She has told Ryan it is too hot for his sweater. Ryan doesn't believe her, so she lets him go.

4. Why does Ryan come back home?
   He is too hot in his sweater.

129

Answer Key

Page 131

Vocabulary Skills

You will find the words below in **bold** print in the article. Find the words and read carefully. Then, write the meaning of each word.

1. shearing _cutting the sheep's hair_
2. fleece _the wool from a sheep_
3. carded _combed_
4. spinning _twisting the wool_

Add **'s** to show that a thing belongs to someone or something. Write the new words.

5. The wool belongs to the sheep.
   It is the _sheep's_ wool.
6. The oil belongs to the fleece.
   It is the _fleece's_ oil.
7. The yarn belongs to the spinner.
   It is the _spinner's_ yarn.

Reading Skills

Write these steps in the correct order.

- Dry the fleece.
- Shear the sheep.
- Card the fleece.
- Spin wool into yarn.
- Wash the fleece.

1. _Shear the sheep._
2. _Wash the fleece._
3. _Dry the fleece._
4. _Card the fleece._
5. _Spin wool into yarn._
6. The author wrote this article to
   _X_ give information.
   _____ make you laugh.
7. Choose the photo you like best. Tell what is happening in the photo.
   Answers will vary.

131

Page 133

Vocabulary Skills

In each row, circle the letters in each word that make the same sound you hear in the underlined word.

jeans feel sweet neat

1. those c(oa)st (ow)ner g(oa)l
2. seeds f(ie)ld wh(ee)l (ea)ger
3. pound cl(ow)n (ou)nce p(ou)t

Look at these words. They are broken into syllables for you. Sound out each syllables. Then, say the words aloud.

4. mechanical
   me / chan / i / cal
5. fabric
   fab / ric
6. separated
   sep / a / rat / ed

Reading Skills

Words such as *it, you,* and *they* take the place of other words. Read these sentences. Then, fill in the blanks.

1. After the cotton is picked, it is cleaned and dried.
   It stands for _cotton_ .
2. Cotton pickers used to wear gloves when they worked.
   They stands for _cotton pickers_
3. Imagine that you are holding a cotton ball. It has many little seeds in it. Does it seem as if it would be easy to get those seeds out? Explain.
   Answers will vary. Ex.: No: if
   the seeds are little, they would
   be all mixed up with the cotton.
4. Before the cotton gin was invented, people had to remove cotton seeds by hand. Would you want that job? Write why or why not.
   Answers will vary.

133

Page 135

Vocabulary Skills

Put a check mark by the meaning that fits the underlined word in each sentence.

1. <u>Well</u>, I thought I looked there.
   _____ a hole for water
   _✓_ a word that people say when they begin speaking
2. The shoes were only a few <u>feet</u> from me.
   _✓_ a unit of measure
   _____ body parts
3. He had to <u>track</u> his shoes to find them.
   _✓_ to follow a trail
   _____ a path
4. He went <u>back</u> into the kitchen.
   _✓_ to go again
   _____ rear part of human body

The missing word in each sentence sounds like *paw*. Change the **p** in *paw* to **cl, gn,** or **r.** Fill in the blanks.

5. I hope Baxter didn't _gnaw_ on the shoes.
6. I think I see a _claw_ mark.
7. Does Baxter like shoes cooked or _raw_ ?

Reading Skills

1. Most stories include a problem. What is this story's problem?
   A boy can't find his
   shoes.
2. As you began to read "Baxter's Shoes," who did you think Baxter was?
   Answers will vary.
3. The **narrator** is the person who tells a story. Whom does the narrator ask for help?
   his mom

135

Page 137

Vocabulary Skills

Read each sentence and circle the word that is made of two shorter words. Write the two words on the lines.

1. A (backyard) practice was just what Andrea needed.
   back _yard_
2. Andrea was more than ready for (kickball) now.
   kick _ball_
3. She learned (something) from her mother.
   some _thing_
4. Playing with mom is okay, but playing with (teammates) is even better.
   team _mates_

Reading Skills

Find words in the story with these meanings.

1. once every twelve months
   yearly
   (Par. 1)
2. find out, get information
   learn
   (Par. 1)
3. area of open ground
   field
   (Par. 3)
4. Andrea is worried because
   she doesn't know how
   to play kickball .
5. Put a check mark by the sentence that best tells about how Andrea looks in the picture.
   _____ Andrea is lazy.
   _____ Andrea thinks kickball is funny.
   _✓_ Andrea is working hard.
6. What lesson did Andrea learn?
   Things work out if
   _____ you keep things to yourself.
   _✓_ you let people help you.
   _____ you never let anyone see you have a problem.

137

Answer Key

Page 139

Vocabulary Skills

Circle the best word for each sentence. Then, write it in the blank.

1. Good exercise will help you ___grow___.
   - (grow)   gray   group

2. Eating many different kinds of foods is ___smart___.
   - smoky   (smart)   smell

3. Slow down, don't eat so ___quickly___.
   - (quickly)   quiet   quilt

The sentences below all have underlined pairs of words that begin with the same letter. One word in each pair is missing. Fill in the blanks.

4. It is important to <u>eat</u> well and <u>exercise</u> to stay healthy.

5. Choose from among the <u>four</u> <u>food</u> groups.

6. Do not snack on <u>sweet</u> or ___salty___ foods between meals.

Reading Skills

1. This article is mostly about what?
   - _____ It is important to eat the right foods.
   - _____ Make sure you exercise every day.
   - __X__ Eat well and exercise to stay healthy.

2. If people don't have time to exercise, what can they do to stay active? Write two ideas.
   - Answers will vary.
   - _____

3. What do you do to stay healthy?
   - Answers will vary.
   - _____
   - _____

139

Page 141

Vocabulary Skills

The missing word in each sentence contains the letters **ow**. Fill in the blanks.

1. I looked out the ___window___ right away.

2. Everything was covered with ___snow___.

3. We jumped down into the ___hollow___.

Circle the three words in each row that belong together.

4. (snow) (rain) grass (hail)
5. fence (hill) (slope) (mountain)
6. (room) time (wall) (floor)
7. (snowman) (fort) (snowbank) shovel

Reading Skills

1. There was no school because ___it had snowed during___ ___the night___.

2. The girls made rooms by <u>pushing their shoulders</u> <u>against the snow</u>.

3. The girls lost track of time, so ___Mom came and got them___.

4. What did the girls add to their snow rooms?
   - ___benches, a door, a___ ___picture___

5. What did Mom do when she came to get the girls?
   - ___She had some snow___ ___lunch with the girls.___

Some of these sentences are about **real** things. Write **R** by them. The other sentences are about **make-believe** things. Write **M** by them.

6. __M__ Snowflakes are magic.
7. __R__ Girls make snow forts.
8. __M__ Snowmen come to life.

141

Page 143

Vocabulary Skills

Fill in each blank with the right pair of letters to make a word.
   - ar   er   ur

1. Bentley was a quiet Vermont f_ar_mer.

2. He worked hard to learn how to take pict_ur_es.

3. He discovered that each snowflake was diff_er_ent.

Circle the word in each pair that has a long vowel sound like the sound in hope.

4. (know)   work
5. (snow)   look
6. discover   (microscope)

Reading Skills

Circle the word or phrase that means the same as the underlined part of each sentence.

1. Bentley <u>discovered</u> that each snowflake is different.
   - (found out)   wondered

2. Even as a boy, Bentley was <u>interested</u> in many things.
   - (curious about)   knew about

3. What did Bentley do when he wasn't looking at snowflakes?
   - He was a farmer.

4. How did Bentley get a good look at snowflakes?
   - He looked at them through a microscope.

5. What is one challenge that Bentley met?
   - Answers will vary.

6. What other challenges might Bentley have met while trying to take pictures of snowflakes?
   - Answers will vary, but might include waiting until winter, keeping the snowflakes cold, working out in the cold.

143

Page 145

Vocabulary Skills

Write the words from the article that have these meanings.

1. lowered and raised the head ___nodded___ (Par. 2)

2. a low, rumbling noise ___growl___ (Par. 3)

3. without noise ___silently___ (Par. 4)

4. to hand something to someone ___pass___ (Par. 6)

Circle the best word for each sentence. Then, write it in the blank.

5. The chicken and the pork ___chops___ were mixed up.
   - charts   chins   (chops)

6. We had hoped for only a ___short___ wait.
   - shape   (short)   shell

A word part that makes one sound is a **syllable**. Words, like *server*, that have two consonants between two vowels, are divided between the consonants: *ser / ver*. Draw a line to divide each word below into syllables.

7. o r / d e r

8. n o d / d e d

Reading Skills

1. This story is mostly about
   - _____ a rude table server.
   - __X__ a family's mixed-up meal.
   - _____ a bad meal at a restaurant.

2. Number the sentences to show what happened first, second, third, and last.
   - __4__ The family passed the food.
   - __2__ The family waited.
   - __3__ The server brought the food.
   - __1__ The server took their orders.

145

Answer Key

Page 147

Vocabulary Skills

Each of these words has an ending. Underline the base words.

1. seems
2. changed
3. server
4. doing

Write the story words that have these meanings.

5. sad

    _____unhappy_____
    (Par. 1)

6. keep in mind

    _____remember_____
    (Par. 2)

7. list of foods

    _____menu_____
    (Par. 2)

8. a person who buys something

    _____customer_____
    (Par. 3)

9. a person who waits on others

    _____server_____
    (Par. 3)

Reading Skills

1. This article is mostly about

    __X__ what a server has to do.

    _____ why servers get mixed up.

    _____ how to act in a restaurant.

2. Name two things that might be hard about being a server. Write why.

    _____Answers will vary._____

    _____

3. If you were a server, what kind of restaurant would you want to work in? Write why.

    _____Answers will vary._____

Number the words to show A-B-C order. If two words have the same first letter, look at the second letter.

4. __2__ remember
   __1__ job
   __4__ server
   __3__ restaurant

147

Page 149

Vocabulary Skills

To show more than one, add **s**. If a word ends in **ch**, add **es**. So, one *inch* becomes two *inches*. Change the endings of these words to show that there are more than one.

1. one match
   two_____matches_____

2. one candle
   two_____candles_____

3. one game
   two_____games_____

4. one watch
   two_____watches_____

Write the word from the story that is the opposite of each word.

5. same   _____different_____
                      (Par. 1)

6. nothing _____everything_____
                        (Par. 2)

7. noisy   _____silent_____
                     (Par. 3)

8. lose   _____win_____
                   (Par. 4)

Reading Skills

1. How did everyone act when the lights went out?

    At first, _everyone was silent_.

    Then, _they all talked at once._

    Finally, _Mom and Dad got candles and matches._

2. Before the lights went out, how did you think the story would turn out?

    _____Answers will vary._____

    _____

3. Did the story turn out how you expected it to? Explain.

    _____Answers will vary._____

    _____

4. How do you think that playing by candlelight was different from playing before the lights went out?

    _____Answers will vary._____

    _____

149

Page 151

Vocabulary Skills

Circle the best word for each sentence. Then, write it in the blank.

1. Have you ever seen an old oil _____lamp_____?

    (**lamp**)   step   bump

2. A _____wick_____ is part of almost all lamps.

    tack   chunk   (**wick**)

3. People used animal _____fat_____ to make lamps for thousands of years.

    part   (**fat**)   hut

Write a word from the story that stands for this pair of words.

4. that is _____that's_____

Now, make a contraction from each pair of words.

5. should not _____shouldn't_____

6. he has _____he's_____

7. she would _____she'd_____

8. it will _____it'll_____

Reading Skills

1. How could someone make a lamp out of a hollow stone?

    _____Answers will vary._____

    _____

2. What else might you have used to make a lamp a very long time ago?

    __X__ an animal horn

    _____ a plastic dish

    _____ a leaf

3. Find the oldest lamp shown on the opposite page. What is it made out of? Write how you think it works.

    _____Answers will vary._____

    _____

4. Look at the second photo. How is this lamp different from the lamp in the first picture?

    _____Answers will vary._____

    _____

151

Notes

Notes

Notes